MURDER & MAYHEM IN HERKIMER COUNTY

EDITED BY CARYL HOPSON AND SUSAN R. PERKINS

THE History PRESS

Published by The History Press
Charleston, SC
www.historypress.com

Images are from the authors' collection unless otherwise stated.

First published 2019

ISBN 9781540241498

Library of Congress Control Number: 20199520042

Notice: The information in this book is true and complete to the best of our knowledge. It is offered without guarantee on the part of the authors or The History Press. The authors and The History Press disclaim all liability in connection with the use of this book.

CONTENTS

Acknowledgements 5
Introduction 7

John Adam Hartmann, the Leatherstocking Man 9
The People Versus Eleven-Year-Old John Bowman 11
The Great Little Falls Bank Robbery 13
Murder Most Diabolical and Atrocious 17
A Drink to Make Up 21
The Murder of Anson Casler 24
The Black Widow of Warren 27
Mashed to Death 29
Murder by the Mansion 31
The Murders of Bellinger and Hayes 33
The Murder of Orlo Davis 37
The Murder of Moses Craig Holden Sr. 40
The John Wishart Murder 42
A Timeless Tragedy 45
The Hanging of a Murderess 49
Murder in Middleville 54
Quarrel Over a Button 57
Vale of Tears 59
Jealous Lover: The Ella Ausman Murder 66
Nellie Had a Date with Death 70
The Case of Infanticide 73

Contents

An Unusual Tragedy 75
Chester Gillette 81
A Rocky Marriage Ends in an Axe Blow 85
Murder on Garden Street 87
Caught on Film 91
A Murder of Forgiveness 96
Arthur W. Wood Murdered in Schuyler 103
The Notorious 1916 Little Falls Trunk Murder 106
The Killing of Henry Werner 109
Lured to Their Deaths: The Mulkoon Affair 115
A Wolf in Sheep's Clothing 119
Wagner-Hotaling Murder of Little Falls 123
The Final Argument 125
The Trespassing Cows 129
The Brewer Mystery 132
Taken for a Ride: Paolo Basile 137
The Last Still Raid 141

Notes 145
Bibliography 147
About the Editors 159

ACKNOWLEDGEMENTS

This book is made possible by the contributions of our authors: Ted Adams, Jane Bellinger, Kelsey Denton, Jane Dieffenbacher, Barbara Dunadee, Faith Eckler, Jim Greiner, Jeffrey Gressler, Mary Haefele, Angela Harris, Caryl and Jim Hopson, David Krutz, Kathy Huxtable, Gregg Lawrence, Peg Masters, Susan Perkins, Fran Peruzzi, Donna Rubin, Jack Sherman, Margaret Sinclair, Jeff Steele, Roberta Walsh, Dennis Webster and Wendy Ladd Weeks. It has been an honor to work with each and every one of them, and we thank them for helping to compile a historical record of homicides and other criminal cases in Herkimer County. We also would like to thank Darryl Grubner for working his editing magic and touching up our images for the book, Iva Trevett for indexing our vertical files on murder cases to help with our research and Herkimer County clerk Sylvia Rowan and the staff at the Herkimer County Clerk's Office for their assistance in locating criminal records for us.

INTRODUCTION

In 1885, after the sensational Roxalana Druse murder case caught everyone's attention in the newspaper headlines, W.H. Tippetts of Herkimer compiled a history on homicides in Herkimer County using court minutes and criminal indictments found at the County Clerk's Office. When the book came out, titled *Murders of Herkimer County*, the *Richfield Springs Mercury* declared in its April 30, 1885 issue, "It is meeting with quite a sale, but why anyone wants to call up such gloomy recollections for, is beyond the understanding of most people." Indeed. Murder cases have always fascinated the public.

We have selected some of the stories found in Tippetts's book and have used resources available to us today to further research these stories and bring new information to light on them. We are also going beyond his book, which ended in 1885, to feature murder cases up to the 1930s. From the collection of former county historian H. Paul Draheim, who did double duty as newspaper reporter and crime scene photographer, we have images of crime scenes never before seen by the public.

But where does the "mayhem" part of the book come in? There are a few sensational crimes that we included that did not involve murder but were too outstanding not to include.

The stories that are presented to you in this publication were contributed by local historians. It is through their research and efforts that we are able to present this book to you today.

JOHN ADAM HARTMANN, THE LEATHERSTOCKING MAN

By Jane M. Bellinger

John Adam Hartmann, who went by Adam, had all the characteristics of a "Leatherstocking Man." This big, powerful built, adventurous frontiersman volunteered as a ranger in the Tryon County Militia and later in the New York Levies during seven years of combat in the War for Independence from 1777 to 1783. Being a fearless Patriot, he became recognized as the most noted of all the Indian fighters on the frontier in the upper valley of the Mohawk River.

Adam's fame became known throughout America and Europe when it was believed that the adventures of the German character Major Hartmann in James Fenimore Cooper's *Leatherstocking Tales* were patterned after this well-known woodsman.

After the war, one of the first court trials for a murder case of an Indian was set, with Adam as the defendant. The incident was told to Frederick Petrie by Hartmann and later recorded in J.P. Simms's *Frontiersmen of New York*. At a little tavern in the eastern part of the present town of Schuyler, a few neighbors would meet in the evenings to smoke, drink a glass of grog and talk over the news. One night, a lone Mohawk Indian known as "Saucy Nick" entered the barroom, spent time at the bar and joined in the conversation of those in the room. Adam had on a green coat, evidence to all but the Indian that it had been a trophy of the war, once worn by one of Johnson's Greens. The Indian, knowing Tories associated with Johnson's company, took Hartmann as one of Johnson's men and directed most of his conversation to him. When the conversation turned to events of the war, the Indian began to boast in broken English of his own cruel deeds. He told of the number of rebels he had killed and scalped and the number of captives he had taken to Canada. When the Indian exhibited his tobacco pouch, made from the skin taken from a white child's arm and tanned, with the nails of the fingers and thumbs still hanging to it, some threatening expression was spoken in German by Hartmann.

The next morning, the Indian again met the man in the green coat. As the two were heading in the same direction, Hartmann very kindly offered to carry his companion's rifle, for the Indian carried a heavy pack and some other treasures. After that day, the Indian was never seen again.

One year later, in the barroom, the subject of the Indian was brought up. Adam was heard to say, "That Indian never got far from here." The expression caused great surprise. Hartmann also said that "the carcass may be found in the little swamp close by, along with his beautiful tobacco pouch." The skeleton of a man, a rusty rifle and a pack with Indian belongings was found. It was said that a former Tory brought the charge of murder against Hartmann. The trial was held at Johnstown, the Tryon County seat, for Herkimer County hadn't been organized yet. With little evidence, Adam was acquitted.

Adam, a well-known and very popular man, was elevated to a place of confidence and trust by the people of the newly formed town of Herkimer when the town was organized in 1788. His name is recorded in "The First Book of Records for Herkimer Town—1789" as one of the overseers of the highways. He had survived the end of the War for Independence by more than fifty-two years, but because of the hardships he endured, before and during the war, Hartmann was an invalid for most of his life. He died in 1836. Reverend John Peter Spinner's death notice, written in Latin, gives a good account of his life. Translated in English, it states, "John Adam Hartmann from the city of Edenkoben in the Palatine district in Germany emigrated at the age of 16 years to the town of Schuyler, Herkimer County. He was a patriot in the War for Independence, suffered many years from rheumatism and for as many as three years he went about with great pain in his side. His age was 92 years and 7 months and he was interred in the cemetery near the church in the village of Herkimer." When the present stone chapel was built at the Reformed Church in 1894, the grave of Hartmann was removed to the Mohawk Cemetery at Mohawk, New York, by his former Shoemaker relations.

THE PEOPLE VERSUS ELEVEN-YEAR-OLD JOHN BOWMAN

By Jeff Steele

"*Atrocious Murder*—We do not recollect of having seen a more wicked and diabolical deed," noted the *Herkimer American* newspaper on July 4, 1811. Exactly one week earlier, eleven-year-old John Bowman had brutally murdered Ann Eliza White, the four-year-old daughter of the couple with whom he was living. Nearly sixteen months later, a jury convicted young Bowman for his crime, and his sentence was death by hanging. In consideration of his age, the New York legislature passed a special act commuting Bowman's punishment to confinement in state prison at hard labor for the rest of his natural life.[1]

John Bowman resided in the village of Herkimer. James and Abigail White moved to this growing community sometime in the decade prior to 1810, and Ann Eliza White was their only child. John began living with the White family during the year prior to the murder.

An unknown motive prompted John Bowman to take the life of Ann Eliza on June 27, 1811, but the murder of the Whites' little girl was particularly gruesome. According to newspapers, Bowman "decoyed her to the bank of the [Mohawk] river, where he procured himself a club, beat her on the head till her skull was broken, and her face lacerated in a most shocking manner."[2] After this horrific act, Bowman concealed her body by throwing it into the river and then went back to the Whites' house and ate his dinner. When James and Abigail began to miss their daughter's presence, they asked young John if he knew where she was, but he denied any knowledge of her whereabouts. The Whites then began to search for their daughter and found her, about four hours after her murder, still in the river where Bowman had left her.

A town constable, John Phillips, and the local coroner came to investigate. The coroner immediately summoned an inquest jury to assist him in determining the cause of Ann Eliza's death. The coroner's jury gave a verdict of "wilful [*sic*] murder by the said John Bowman." While awaiting trial at the Herkimer County Jail, Bowman vanished one day, much to the surprise of Sheriff John Mahon, who immediately organized an ultimately fruitless search for him. A few hours later, though, Bowman nonchalantly walked back through the front door of the jail. When questioned, he told his jailors that "he was tired of the jail and simply went out to take a walk."[3]

When the Court of Oyer and Terminer finally opened on September 14, John Bowman met the men who would help determine his fate: New York Supreme Court justice Smith Thompson, who was to preside over the case; District Attorney Nathan Williams; and Daniel Cady, Bowman's defense counsel. Cady immediately had John Bowman plead not guilty at his arraignment before Justice Thompson.

John Bowman was in a legal no-man's-land because he was too old for the court to consider him an infant, yet at the same time he was clearly not reasoning as an adult. Further adding urgency to his situation was the fact that the penalty for murder in New York State was still execution. There were a number of penal reforms beginning to sweep America, but there were no statutes yet for youth offenders. The jury, following a trial lasting a single day, convicted him of murder. Justice Thompson then turned to young Bowman and announced that he was "to be hanged by the neck until dead, on the fourth day of December next."[4]

Smith Thompson wrote a letter to Governor Daniel D. Tompkins regarding John Bowman's sentence. He explained to Tompkins that while there was "clear and conclusive" evidence of Bowman's guilt, considering the boy's "tender years," it might be "expedient to arrest his execution by an exchange of punishment." He hoped that Tompkins would bring young Bowman's plight before the legislature, as governors then did not have the power to pardon. In Governor Tompkins's address to the state legislature, most of his speech was on the outbreak of the War of 1812, yet he told the legislators that Bowman's plight was "the only matter of an extraordinary nature which I shall at present press upon your notice."[5]

The state legislature formed a special committee to consider the legal ramifications of commuting Bowman's death sentence. On November 10, the very first act the Thirty-Sixth Session of the New York legislature passed was "An Act Directing the Confinement of John Bowman in the State-Prison at Hard Labor for Life."

Sheriff Mahon brought John Bowman to Newgate Prison in 1812, a far from ideal place to house a young prisoner, but there were no other options for the state to incarcerate Bowman. On February 5, 1821, he died of tuberculosis, which he undoubtedly contracted in Newgate's deplorably overcrowded conditions. The prison was closed in 1828.

In the years after the legislature sent John Bowman to prison, many of those who were involved in some aspect of his case went on to great personal success. Justice Smith Thompson and Governor Daniel D. Tompkins both became part of President James Monroe's administration from 1817 to 1825, with Tompkins serving as Monroe's vice president and Thompson as the secretary of the navy until Monroe appointed him an associate justice on the United States Supreme Court in 1823.[6] Bowman's defense attorney, Daniel Cady, later served in the United States House of Representatives from 1815 to 1817. His daughter was Elizabeth Cady Stanton, one of the most prominent women's rights activists in nineteenth-century America.

THE GREAT LITTLE FALLS BANK ROBBERY

By James Greiner

Albert G. Story was the head cashier at the Herkimer County Bank in Little Falls. On the night of September 25, 1841, Anson C. Brown, a clerk at the same bank, called on him and asked a favor. As it was almost 8:00 p.m., the twenty-one-year-old clerk explained that he had just received two small checks and was wondering if he might be able to get into the bank. He went on to tell Story that he and his brother were planning on going to Utica for the weekend and needed the money. Story never gave it a second thought. Young Brown had been with the bank for several years, having enjoyed "the finest confidence of its officers." Story presented the key to the front door of the bank to Brown, and fifteen minutes later it was back in his possession.[7]

The next day, the Brown family made a startling discovery. Their son Anson was gone, but in his bedroom he left behind a canvas bag containing more money than they had ever seen. They immediately contacted Albert G. Story, and he in turn contacted the Sheriff's Department in the village of Herkimer.

Story related to Deputy Sheriff John D. Livingston the events of the previous evening. The banker and the lawman came to the same conclusion. This was a classic "inside job" bank robbery. Once Anson Brown was in the bank, he used another set of keys to open the vault. Since he was familiar with the contents of the vault, he knew what bags to take. Still, it would have been impossible for him to get out of the bank vault, relock the bank door and return the key to Albert G. Story in fifteen minutes. Anson Brown couldn't have done this without help. Livingston later learned that Tobias Green and William C. Franciscus were partners in this crime.

Herkimer County Bank—now the home of the Little Falls Historical Society.

The leading newspaper in Little Falls, the *Mohawk Courier*, was absolutely livid when it discovered that its foreman of the last three years, Tobias Green, was one of the bank robbers. The *Courier* had a difficult time coming to terms with the entire affair. Green had served his apprenticeship with the paper, "and during that period, has enjoyed, in an eminent degree, the confidence of his employer, and the respect and esteem of all those who knew him." According to the paper, Green's involvement in this bank robbery "blasted his reputation forever, engraven upon his brow the indelible mark of felon," and will most likely "spend the flower of his youth and the dawn of manhood within the gloomy walls of prison and among the outcasts of society."[8]

The *Mohawk Courier* couldn't understand how Tobias Green and Anson Brown, who came from "the most respectable families," could rob the bank. They must have come under the influence of someone else, someone like William Franciscus.

The past summer, Franciscus, a journeyman printer, had worked for the *Courier*. The editors of the paper recalled that he was from Baltimore and had once published a newspaper in Nashville, Tennessee. Since he was an outsider, one who had traveled extensively about the country, he was immediately cast as the ringleader. "He has," recorded the *New York Herald*, "a sinister expression of countenance—has travelled much—is artful, licentious in morals, passionate, and intemperate." It was Franciscus who, "seduced by association and intimacy," lured Brown and Green "into irregularities and finally in the perpetuation of [the] crime."[9]

Meanwhile, at the bank, it didn't take Story and his clerks long to realize the magnitude of the heist. At least five bags of cash in all denominations and assorted bank notes, amounting to $68,885, were missing. Added to this was a bag containing $2,332 in gold coins and another that contained $150 in silver coins. The cash and coin totaled $71,357. The greatest concern to the bank was the sheer number of gold coins that were missing. There was always a chance that some out-of-county banks or businesses would not accept bank notes if they didn't know the individual passing the notes. Gold, however, was different. Gold was the best money you could possess, as it was accepted anytime anywhere (hence the expression "good as gold").

When residents of Little Falls learned of the robbery of the Herkimer County Bank, it had the effect of a fire bell in the night. The trustees of the bank met there to assess the situation and were both horrified and frightened. Returning confidence to the banking industry after the Bank Panic of 1837 had taken years. If the money were lost or unrecovered, it could cause a bank panic in Little Falls, resulting in a "run on the bank." Nothing could stop the depositors from going to the bank and trying to withdraw their funds. The trustees knew that a collapse of the bank was on the horizon if the money were not returned, as they could never pay their depositors what was due them.

There was no shortage of volunteers when Deputy Sheriff John D. Livingston said, "Saddle up" and formed a posse. By horse, buggy and wagon, the citizens of Little Falls scoured the back roads, hoping to catch the bandits who had stolen their money. Among them was a local businessman named Horace M. Burch. While the others canvassed the roads leading out of Little Falls, Burch and Livingston went to the train station. Livingston recalled an interesting bit of information when he had spoken to Albert Story earlier that day. Story said that Anson C. Brown mentioned that he needed to cash a few checks because he and his brother were going to Utica. Livingston and Burch agreed that this didn't seem right. Why would anyone want to escape to Utica? What next, Syracuse? The robbers, they correctly deduced, weren't going west—they were headed east to Albany. From there they could either go to New York City or flee the country to Canada.

When Burch and Livingston arrived at the Albany train station, it was almost nightfall. The ticket master said that men matching the description of the fugitives had gotten off the train but that they had left the station. This was good news. Not only were the bank robbers in Albany, but they also hadn't purchased any additional train tickets. Either they were waiting until the next morning to get tickets or they were making plans to leave by horse. With the help of the Albany police, Burch and Livingston located the livery stable that had sold a pair of horses and a hack to the robbers.

Once more, the pursuers had to determine in which direction to give chase. The most logical thing to do was to take the southbound train that led to New York City. From the great port, they could go almost anywhere. Although the police were aware that the robbers didn't buy train tickets, as a precaution, the next they day scouted the roads leading south out of Albany. They satisfied themselves that the bank robbers didn't escape this way. They were on their way to Canada.

Meanwhile, Burch and Livingston were pushing their horses as hard as they could on the road that led to Saratoga Springs. Apparently, the robbers were doing the exact same thing. Their luck finally ran out when one of the horses foundered. The men had to abandon the wagon and walk six miles to a tavern. Our three Little Falls desperados spent the night at the tavern, unaware of the fact that the law was closing in on them. The next morning, they boarded the northbound stagecoach.

The slow-moving stagecoach had gone only a few miles when the driver noticed a cloud of dust in the distance. Several men on horseback were headed right toward his coach. The stagecoach driver reined his team to a halt at about the same time the horsemen pulled alongside and drew their guns. The stage driver must have breathed a sigh of relief when he discovered that these men were not bandits but lawmen. Inside the coach, there was no sigh of relief. When told that resistance was futile, the trio surrendered their guns and bags of money. Only $400 was missing.[10]

Brown, Green and Franciscus were taken back to Albany and, from there, boarded the train for Herkimer. There was no plea bargaining in those days or a "this is my first offence" defense for the trio. Each pleaded guilty and was sentenced to "four years confinement at hard labor" at Auburn State Prison.[11]

MURDER MOST DIABOLICAL AND ATROCIOUS

By Faith W. Eckler

Thusly was the murder that took place on the night of February 23, 1850, described by the *Mohawk Courier*. It was dark and cold. The snow lay ten or twelve inches deep on the ground as a young man, about twenty-five years of age, trudged down the road from Newport. He was about five feet, nine inches tall and was warmly dressed for the weather in a black broadcloth coat with outside pockets; dark-blue cassimere (cashmere) pants; a worsted vest of mouse-colored background, striped or plaid with white and blue; a linen shirt; and yellow buckskin drawers. In his pocket was a blue handkerchief with white spots, and around his waist he wore a money belt.

The young man was a peddler, and he carried with him a pack, now nearly empty, and a tin box. He was on his way to Utica to replenish his stock. He was accompanied by another man, who wore a plush cap and a light-colored coat. The two had been traveling together for quite a distance when the second man apparently convinced the peddler to take a shortcut to another road from Newport through the fields of farmer James Van Vleck of Schuyler. A third man who was passing through the neighborhood about 9:00 p.m. heard sounds of a struggle proceeding from a nearby haystack about one mile from the road. He heard a plea for mercy answered by the cry, "There, damn you; you've got enough." Supposing that a fight was in progress, he didn't stop to investigate, not wanting to get involved.

The body of the peddler was discovered six days later on March 1 in a lot near Knapp's tavern, about five miles from Utica. It was a grisly scene. The corpse had sustained four stab wounds—two in the neck, nearly severing the head; one in the breast; and another in the abdomen. Great quantities of blood had melted the snow down to the ground around the body. There was no sign of the peddler's pack or tin box. His boots and hat were also missing. His pockets had been turned inside out, and the only money found on his body was two cents.

The murder instantly became a sensation in this peaceable area, where such crimes were virtually nonexistent, and the investigation was exhaustively reported in the local newspapers. Coroner Dygert removed the body to Frankfort, and an attempt was begun to establish the peddler's identity. The only clue was the initials "E.K." found on articles of the victim's clothing. Several citizens, upon seeing the body, expressed a very confident belief that it was that of Mr. Angel of Newport, but this proved not to be the case.

William H. Pratt of Deerfield testified at the inquest that the murdered man had recently called at his house in the company of another man and that he believed him to be a German Jew. Regarding his companion, Pratt testified that he asked for a drink, but the peddler, not being a drinking man, asked for a cigar instead.

Within a few days, a committee of Jews from Utica requested the body for burial. Just as they were making plans for the interment, a German arrived in Frankfort who recognized the deceased as a man he had met some days earlier at Sprakers. He added that the man had two brothers living at Fultonville, Montgomery County. It was not until March 21 that the *Utica Daily Gazette* announced that the victim's name was Kline.

Meanwhile, the authorities had found a suspect. The *Herkimer Democrat* of March 8 reported:

> *The murderer is supposed, from any suspicious circumstances, to be one John Allen who lives about ¾ mile from the place where the horrid crime was perpetrated. Allen was recently married in Schuyler where he was but slightly known. He left his home and has recently been traced to this place* [Herkimer] *where he took the cars and can be easily identified, having a felon* [an inflammation] *over one of his eyes* [as a result of which, it was reported that he frequently kept his hat well down on his forehead]. *He was considered a suspicious character by his neighbors. Deputy sheriff James Foltz is in pursuit of him, accompanied by Mr. Straus of Frankfort. They started 24 hours behind him.*

The *Utica Daily Observer* provided more details:

> *Deputy Sheriff Foltz of Frankfort, accompanied by a German peddler of jewelry named Levinger, is in full and close pursuit of a man named Allen whom it is said, they have strong reason to suspect committed the recent murder in Schuyler. We learn that Allen resided in the Town of Deerfield and has conducted himself very strangely since the murder. It is said that he was present at the inquest, but refused to look at the body and soon left; that he had been seen with a peddler's box like the one carried by the deceased; that he had lately been quite restless, staying away from his home…and, lastly, that he called at the Rail Road office in Herkimer to purchase a ticket for Little Falls…and while doing so, exhibited to the R.R. agent a number of gold pieces, eagles, doubloons, &c, inquiring their value.…Allen is known as a poor man.*

Allen was quickly apprehended, and by March 11, he was lodged in the Herkimer County Jail awaiting a hearing. The hearing began March 15 at the courthouse in Herkimer before Judges McCauley, Rasbach and Putnam. The courthouse was crowded with spectators and witnesses. The body was present as well. District Attorney George A. Judd appeared for the people and Samuel and Robert Earl for the prisoner. Allen was identified as an Irishman who had lived in England for a long time. He was twenty-nine years of age, had served in the British army for seven years and had been married in England, although it was rumored that his wife was dead. Warner D. Cane told the court that he had first seen the prisoner about six weeks previously, when he had married him to Purdy Ann Gilbert, a widow. He believed that Allen had lived in St. Johnsville, where he worked on a farm for eight months, and that he had emigrated from England about eighteen months before the incident. William Pratt testified that he knew Allen and that he was not the man who had accompanied the peddler to his house.

Considerable testimony centered on the pack that Allen had been carrying when he was apprehended. Was it the same as that of the peddler? Some witnesses said it was larger; others said that it was smaller. Michael Gaffney of Utica, a dealer in peddler's goods, said that he had viewed the pack at the Herkimer County Jail and that it contained items that he recognized from his store. Edward Manning, Gaffney's clerk, said that the accused had visited the store and made a number of purchases. He flashed a roll of bills containing several two-dollar notes and at least two or three five-dollar notes. He appeared agitated, Manning testified, and kept chewing tobacco and spitting it out.

Dr. Paul Devendorf described the scene when Allen was brought to see the corpse. Devendorf asked Allen to lay his hand on the body, and he did so. The doctor asked him if he could see any wounds that would produce death. Allen pointed out two. The doctor then asked him if he could see any others. The prisoner seized the hair of the peddler's head and said that he saw another wound on the neck. Devendorf pressed him to look still further, and Allen lifted up the head and pointed to the gash on the back of the peddler's neck. He remarked that it was a shocking affair. Dr. Devendorf asked Allen how he happened to look at those particular places. The prisoner replied that he had heard of the crime but could not remember who had told him.

Perhaps the most damaging testimony came from Abraham Conklin of Newport, for he put Allen at the scene of the murder on the day in question. Conklin said that he had had a conversation with Allen about the murder. Allen insisted that he could prove himself innocent. He alleged that he and an Englishman named Heath had started across Van Vleck's field well before sunset. According to Allen, they came to a gulf where Heath stopped, but Allen proceeded on to his home, arriving about sunset. Conklin informed him that Mrs. Allen had reported that her husband never came home that night. According to Conklin, this news seemed to agitate the accused, but he continued to assert that he could prove that he was at Van Vleck's before sunset. Apparently, he was never asked to do so, and several witnesses testified that they knew of no Englishman named Heath.

The hearing concluded on Saturday afternoon, March 16, and Allen was committed for trial at the next sitting of the circuit court, to be held at Herkimer in early April. At that time, he was arraigned and pleaded not guilty. Little new evidence was presented that had not been disclosed at the preliminary hearing. Allen languished in the Herkimer County Jail until September 4, when he came up for trial before Judge Philo Gridley of Utica, justice of the Supreme Court of the Fifth District; Ezra Graves, county judge; and David Humphrey and Morgan S. Churchill, justices of the sessions. Once again, District Attorney Judd presented the prosecution case, assisted by Hiram Nolton of Little Falls. Thirty-nine witnesses were called, but no new solid evidence was produced. The entire people's case appeared to be based on circumstantial evidence and speculation. The prosecution rested at 5:00 p.m. on September 5.

Allen was again represented by Samuel and Robert Earl of Utica, as well as Volney Owen of Mohawk. The defense rose to call its one and only witness, Deputy Sheriff Howard, who testified to the finding of a pair of gloves concealed in the home of a man at Deerfield who had been arrested for stealing horses. These gloves bore the same initials as those found on the clothes of the murdered peddler. Here, the defense rested.

The *Utica Daily Observer* reported the verdict:

> *After commending the diligence of the people's counsel, Col. Judd, that whom there is probably not a more thorough and indefatigable District Attorney in the whole state, the court expressed the unanimous opinion that the prosecution had failed to criminally connect the prisoner with the crime for which he was arraigned, and the jury agreeing, John Allen was at once acquitted and discharged from custody.*
>
> *The prisoner who had maintained great composure during the trial, burst into tears when the decision of the court was pronounced and appeared deeply affected. At this moment a little incident occurred worth adding. One of the spectators on the back seats* [elsewhere described as tall

> and rough-looking] *who had hitherto attracted no attention, and with a voice suffocated by his feelings, asked the court if he could say a word. After a moment's hesitation, the court said he might, when, with a heart overflowing with sympathy for his comrade and a professional pride at his acquittal, he exclaimed, "I've known that man sixteen years; he served with me in the army; I know that he has always borne a good character." The interesting moment at which this statement was volunteered and the earnest emotion with which it was delivered sent a shrill* [sic] *through the whole house, and constituted stronger vindication of the general character of the accused than would volumes of deliberate eulogy. All seemed satisfied that the trial resulted in the acquittal of the prisoner.*

The newspaper accounts do not give the name of the horse thief, nor do they relate whether he (or anyone else) was subsequently indicted for the peddler's murder. The following item from the *Utica Gazette* of August 24, 1850, is, however, intriguing. Under the headline "Horse Thief Caught," it was reported, "Officers Deming and Hess arrested James P. Stickney near Deerfield Corners last Thursday on a charge of having stolen a horse and wagon in New Hampshire on the 13th inst." Was it at Stickney's house that the gloves were found? Was he the real killer? Or did Allen get away with murder?

A DRINK TO MAKE UP

By Kathy Huxtable

To share a drink or not—that is a serious question, especially when the other person has sworn to kill you. George Platts owned a small plot of land in the town of Litchfield, but he often needed to work out on neighboring farms to support his wife and five children. He occasionally worked for Miles Wilcox, who had a much larger farm. For some reason, Wilcox began to suspect that Platts was a little "too intimate" with Wilcox's wife, Mercy. This caused several quarrels between the two men. Wilcox threatened to shoot Platts and ordered him never to set foot in his house again.

Platts kept his distance for a considerable length of time, and in June 1860, the men appeared to rebuild their friendship. Wilcox stated that he no longer believed that his suspicions and the stories that had circulated about Platts and his wife were true. Platts again began to work on the Wilcox farm and visit at the house.

On August 15, 1860, Platts worked for Wilcox, but he did not return home until the next morning. He told his wife, Caroline, that he and Wilcox had argued all night. The following weekend was the occasion of a community picnic and dance held near Jerusalem Hill in Litchfield. Platts was in charge of the dance. Witnesses reported that Platts was sober, but Wilcox seemed rather intoxicated. During the festivities, the men began to quarrel again. At some point, Wilcox called a halt to the arguing and suggested that they "drink and make up," offering a bottle of liquor.

Platts took a drink and yelled, "Wilcox, you have poisoned me!" "You can't prove it," replied Wilcox. Platts began to walk home, falling several times. He collapsed at his house, telling his wife that Wilcox had poisoned him. Before any medical help arrived, he was dead. Meanwhile, Wilcox also started to exhibit symptoms of poisoning. As he was found with two bottles in his pocket, some assumed that due to his intoxication, he had mistakenly taken a sip from the wrong bottle. Others thought that he had become remorseful and tried to do away with himself. He did, however, receive medical attention and was later taken home. Rumor circulated that because he also thought he would die, he confessed to his family.

A postmortem exam of Platts on Sunday resulted in a suspicion of poisoning. By Monday, Wilcox, still feeling ill, was arrested and moved to the Herkimer County Jail. Several physicians called for an inquest, removed Platts's stomach and sent it to Albany for medical and chemical examination. After Platts was buried, a further request was received from Albany to exhume the body, remove the lungs, kidneys and liver and deliver those organs for examination also. The resulting analysis revealed the presence of strychnine in considerable quantities.

At the coroner's trial, a witnesses stated that on August 9, a man called at the drugstore of Smith & Hall in Utica and asked for strychnine but did not obtain it. On August 20, a man, identified as A.M. Smith of Litchfield, called at another drugstore—Dickinson, Comstock & Company, also in Utica—and purchased a small quantity of strychnine. Mr. Dickinson positively identified Wilcox as that man. In the face of overwhelming evidence, the coroner's jury reached the verdict that George G. Platts died by means of strychnine, administered to him by Miles Wilcox, with intent to kill. Wilcox was indicted for murder in April 1861.

It wasn't until late October 1861 that the trial began before circuit judge Joseph Mullin. Roscoe Conkling, a rising young lawyer and U.S. congressman from Utica, served as Wilcox's attorney, with S.S. Morgan as the prosecuting district attorney. Conkling had recently finished an astonishing, medically oriented defense in the murder trial of Reverend Henry Budge in Rome and was now a much sought-after attorney for serious criminal cases. A skilled orator and an imposing figure in a courtroom, he proved to be a great asset to Wilcox.

It seemed to be a clear-cut case of murder in the first. Wilcox originally pleaded not guilty, but Conkling was able to find a way for that plea to be withdrawn and allow Wilcox to plead guilty to the lesser charge of manslaughter in the third degree. Judge Mullin was furious and refused to accept the new plea but was overruled by the county judge and the justices of sessions. Wilcox received a sentence of two years and six months at Auburn State Prison, a rather light punishment that did not sit well with the public.

Auburn prison records indicate that Wilcox was sentenced on November 8, 1861, served his time and was released in May 1864 with money in his pocket, earned while doing work at Auburn. On August 12, 1864, the governor of New York, Horatio Seymour, signed an order to restore all rights of citizenship to Miles Wilcox. It is interesting to note that Governor Seymour just happened to be the brother-in-law of Roscoe Conkling.

Mercy Wilcox was a woman who apparently stood by her man, as the 1865 New York State census shows the Wilcox family, consisting of Miles, Mercy and their four children living on a farm that they owned in Cherry Creek, Chautauqua County. By 1870, the family was now farming in the town of Dayton, Cattaraugus County, and another child had joined the family. However, Miles died in 1871, cause unknown. Was it possible that his death was the result of a lingering effect of the strychnine? Mercy did eventually remarry, although when she died in 1905, she was buried beside Miles at the Cottage Cemetery in Cattaraugus County.

The loss of her husband, George, was not the only tragedy that Caroline Schooley Platts suffered. A year after the trial, her sixteen-year-old son, Montraville, enlisted in the Union army and served with the 152nd New York Infantry. He was declared missing in action after the first battle of Weldon's Railroad near Petersurgh, Virginia, in June 1864 and later appeared on the list of deceased at Andersonville Prison. Caroline never remarried, died in 1900 and was buried with her husband at the Kinne Cemetery in Litchfield.

THE MURDER OF ANSON CASLER

By David Krutz

On Tuesday morning, September 18, 1865, the lifeless body of Anson Casler was pulled from the Erie Canal in Little Falls between Locks 38 and 39. A preliminary autopsy performed by Dr. Silas Ingham revealed that Casler had contusions over his right eye and on the bridge of his nose and a significant wound at the base of his skull that may have broken his neck.

Dr. Ingham believed that the wounds were caused by a fist or an iron rod. He also concluded that these wounds, and not drowning, were the cause of Casler's death. A subsequent coroner's inquest agreed with Dr. Ingham's conclusion and found that Anson Casler came to his death "by the hands of some person or persons unknown."

Thirty-year-old Anson Casler, a constable in the village of Little Falls's police force, was "a young man of most temperate character, mild disposition, indisposed to quarrel, and was generally esteemed for his excellent habits and quiet demeanor." He lived with his brother, Marcus, on Casler Street, where they operated a livery business. His murder, which was reported in numerous newspapers from Syracuse to Albany, is believed to be the only death of an on-duty Little Falls policeman.

The night before the discovery of his body, Constable Casler had attempted to serve an arrest warrant on nineteen-year-old Edward Fleming, who lived in a rooming house on Mohawk Street, a short distance from where Casler's body was found. That afternoon, Fleming had beaten Calvin Angus on Main Street in Little Falls with an iron cane. The cane had been given to him by his friend, seventeen-year-old John Foster. Police attention immediately turned to Fleming and Foster.

As was expected, Edward Fleming became the prime suspect in the killing of Anson Casler. When questioned, Fleming didn't deny that he had beaten Calvin Angus with an iron cane, but after the fight, he had given the cane back to John Foster. He had then returned home and, in a drunken stupor, went to bed. His alibi was corroborated by his sister, Mrs. Catherine Vaughn.

The Little Falls police investigation then focused on John Foster. Foster stated that he knew nothing about the murder of Casler and that he was well acquainted with the constable and had never had any trouble with him. Foster readily turned over the iron cane to Constable Henry Ritter. At this point, the questioning of John Foster ended because the sheriff of Orleans County arrived in Little Falls and arrested Foster for "horse thievery." Subsequently, Foster was sentenced to three years' imprisonment in Auburn State Prison.

Without substantial evidence of Fleming's involvement in the murder and with Foster gone, the Casler murder case went cold. But after lying dormant for six years, it burst back onto the scene in 1871 when Joseph Schuyler revealed that he knew who had killed Anson Casler.

Joseph Schuyler, a resident of the town of Danube, was no model citizen. At age seventeen, he was arrested for robbery and sent to prison. In 1863, he was charged with attempted rape, convicted and returned to Auburn prison for three more years. According to Schuyler, he was acquainted with both Anson Casler and John Foster. While serving his second term in Auburn, he often conversed with John Foster. On one occasion, Foster told him that he and Edward Fleming had killed Anson Casler because Casler had a "warrant on them." Foster reportedly said, "We hit him on the head with an iron cane and threw his body in the canal."

In the early months of 1871, Schuyler met with the Herkimer County district attorney Albert Mills and, under oath, signed a sworn statement detailing Foster's jailhouse confession. Based on Schuyler's affidavit, warrants for the arrest of Edward Fleming and John Foster were issued. Foster was arrested in Detroit and extradited to Herkimer, and Fleming was also taken into custody.

The Court of Oyer and Terminer trial of John Foster opened in Herkimer to a packed house on Wednesday, July 5, 1871, with the Honorable C.H. Doolittle presiding. After opening statements, the prosecution called its witnesses. After testimony on the events leading up to the issuance of the Fleming warrant, various witnesses recounted the movements of Anson Casler on his fateful night and the search for and recovery of his body. Dr. Ingham next detailed the results of the autopsies.

In an attempt to show animosity between the victim and the accused, Marcus Casler testified that a few nights prior to the murder, John Foster had come to his livery stable asking to rent a horse, but Anson had refused Foster and told him to never come there again. Deputy Sheriff Bentley closed the day by attesting that on the day that Casler's body was found, blood was observed on Foster's coat.

On the trial's second day, the prosecution's witnesses related their accounts of the behaviors of Fleming and Foster on the evening of the murder. Fannie Angus stated that John Foster showed her the iron cane and proudly said that it had already been wrapped around one man's head and would be wrapped around another's before the day was over. Nancy Guile

The cemetery marker for Anson Casler.

swore that before the discovery of Casler's body, Foster had told her that the constable had been murdered by four men in capes and hoods. The prosecution's key witness, Joseph Schuyler, closed the day's proceedings with Foster's alleged Auburn prison confession.

The defense team took center stage on the third day of the trial, with the majority of the witnesses providing alibis for the whereabouts of Foster and Fleming during the time that Casler was thought to have been killed. However, under cross-examination, a number of the defense witnesses gave contradictory or vague responses. Daniel Hill testified that Joseph Schuyler was drunk when he signed the prosecution's affidavit, and Seth Richmond, a former Herkimer County sheriff and a prominent Little Falls citizen, defended the reputation of John Foster.

As the last witness, John Foster took the stand. He denied any part in the killing of Casler and noted that, until a few weeks previous, he had never met Joseph Schuyler and certainly had never had any jailhouse conversation with him. Under prolonged cross-examination, he stuck to his story, proclaiming his innocence.

Saturday morning, July 8, 1871, began with closing arguments by each side. The twelve-man jury retired and returned two hours later with the verdict: not guilty. John Foster and Edward Fleming were immediately set free. With those two words, the murder of Constable Anson Casler began to fade from view. Foster and Fleming left the stage, and the trail for Casler's killers went cold. There were no other suspects, and there never had been. The only tangible reminder of that sad day in Little Falls history is the granite gravestone of Anson Casler at Church Street Cemetery.

Note: Through the efforts of the Little Falls Historical Society and the Little Falls Police Department, the name of Anson Casler was added to the fallen Police Officers' Memorial in Albany on May 8, 2018.

THE BLACK WIDOW OF WARREN

By Susan Perkins

Nancy Congdon Yates Gardner Lyman was born in Massachusetts, the daughter of Joseph Congdon. Her family moved to Sharon, Schoharie County, New York, when she was three years old. Nancy then moved to Jordanville. She lived with the family of Collins Warner in the 1830s. Nancy married her first husband, George Yates, circa 1838, when she was eighteen years old. They had six children, and by 1869, only two were living. George had enlisted in the Civil War on January 24, 1863, and was discharged on April 13, 1863, for a disability. He died circa 1864.

On January 18, 1869, Nancy's daughter went to work at Mr. Van Slyk's tavern near Jordanville. Here the daughter became acquainted with Ephraim Gardner, whose wife, Catherine, had died on February 23, 1867. Ephraim and the daughter visited Nancy Yates to propose marriage. She accepted, and Nancy and Ephraim were married that January. In the meantime, Frederick Lyman, another widower, was seeing Nancy. Ephraim began to be violently sick and soon died on March 10, 1869.

Nancy settled the estate in one week. She then married Frederick Lyman, who was seventy-five years old, on April 27, 1869. Suspicions of foul play circulated among the townsfolk. Mr. Gardner's body was disinterred from Dennison Corners Cemetery, and his stomach was taken to Albany for further medical examination. It was determined that he died of arsenic poisoning. Nancy Lyman was arrested and put in the Herkimer County Jail. She had bought the package of arsenic at George Bell's store in Jordanville to kill rats. She claimed that she was innocent and that her husband drank liquor from a bottle that was the same color as the arsenic bottle.

Nancy was found not guilty. A quote in the *Herkimer County Citizen*, May 14, 1869, stated, "Guilty or not, we are rather glad she is not to be hung, for as Lord Mansfield has said, 'Hanging'...especially a woman is the worst use you can put a man to." Two of the jurors were reported as saying they "believed her guilty, only the evidence was not strong enough and she was a woman, as it would be hard to hang her."

What happened to Nancy—or, better yet, Frederick? They remained married for about ten more years, living in the town of Warren until Frederick's death circa 1879 in his late eighties. It is interesting to note that he had made a will on November 9, 1869, the year of their marriage, leaving the majority of his property to his daughter, Miranda Curtis, and the remainder of his property to his son, Leonard. There was no mention of Nancy. Was he safeguarding himself from a similar fate as Ephraim Gardner, or was it at the encouragement of his children?

By the 1880 census, Nancy was listed as a widow in the town of Warren at the age of fifty-eight. She moved to the town of Maine in Broome County in the southern part of the state, where she married for a fourth time to John H. Brooks on March 25, 1883. Nothing more can be found about her, except for a notice of her death in the town of Maine in the *Broome Republican*, dated May 20, 1899. She died on May 13, 1899, according to the New York State Death Index on Ancestry.com. Where she is buried is unknown.

MASHED TO DEATH

By Katherine Huxtable

Nancy Sprague, widowed at a young age and struggling to raise her children alone, made one mistake that cost her dearly. Her friends and neighbors considered her a responsible woman, although she suffered from a nervous temperament and delicate health. Her first husband, Lucian Sprague, who was reported to have died in the army in 1866, left her $2,000 of insurance money. Wisely, Nancy used the funds to buy a small house and barn situated on three acres of land near the old red schoolhouse and the dry dock between Frankfort and Ilion. There she resided with her five children, using the remaining cash to support them.

A town of Columbia native, Dyer (Jedediah) Pangburn, possibly attracted by Nancy's apparent wealth, came on the scene and convinced her to marry him in September 1870. At the age of sixty-six, he was considerably older than Nancy, who was about forty. He had three grown children of his own who lived in the area. Perhaps she hoped he would help raise and support her family.

Dyer Pangburn had some redeeming qualities; he was not a drunkard, and as a day laborer, he was industrious when he worked. However, he had a past, having been convicted of bigamy in Wayne County and committed to the Auburn prison for a two-year sentence in May 1858. Prior to this marriage, he was said to have had anywhere from two to four other wives, some obviously at the same time. Because of this practice, neighbors considered him a Mormon.

Nancy's friends felt that the marriage was doomed from the start. Dyer moved in with Nancy and soon encouraged her to sell the property, ostensibly to give him the proceeds. Stories were told of household items, even sacks of flour, being labeled "His" and "Hers." Arguments were often heard by the neighbors. By December of that year, Nancy had had enough, threw him out and filed for divorce. He continued to return, and in desperation to be rid of him, she threw scalding water on him. He accused her of assault. They eventually made a truce of sorts, and she allowed him back in the house.

In April 1871, Nancy had confided to her doctor that she feared for her life, and soon after, she made a will, designating that all of her property be given to her children and none to Dyer. This may have been the last straw as far as he was concerned.

The night of August 15, 1871, Nancy complained of feeling unwell and said that she would sleep downstairs. She asked Dyer to sleep upstairs. He refused and laid down on the floor near the doorway to the front room. Nancy slept with her eldest daughter, Mary, age ten. Two younger girls, Nancy and Allie, slept on the floor. Her two sons, Harvey and George, ages twelve and thirteen, did not stay at home during the crop season, as they worked and lived elsewhere. Sometime during the night, the girls were awakened by the screams of their mother in the kitchen. Allie ran to Mary and said, "Dyer is killing Ma."

At the kitchen door, Mary and Allie saw their mother, lying on the floor, while Dyer was pounding on her about the head and face with a potato masher. He spotted the girls standing there and warned them that he would do the same to them if they didn't leave. Mary recalled that they were horrified, ran back to the bed and pulled the covers over their heads. They heard Dyer continue to beat on their mother and then pace about; at last, he opened and shut the outside door and left. Still terrified, the girls huddled in their bed for hours until daylight. Only then did they climb out a window and run to a neighbor's house.

The neighbors quickly sounded the alarm. The horrific scene they found in the kitchen was beyond comprehension—blood splattered everywhere, including the walls, and the body of Mrs. Pangburn, covered in blood, disfigured and crumpled on the floor. The apparent murder weapon, the bloody potato masher, lay beside her on the floor. At once the men began to search for the perpetrator, whom the children had stated to be Dyer Pangburn. They did not have to search far. Hanging from a rafter in the small barn was Dyer's limp and cold body, an apparent suicide.

Mary testified at the coroner's inquest, stating that she did not know of any argument between her mother and Dyer that day, although they did argue the previous day. She said that she had never seen Dyer strike her mother before but that she witnessed several blows during the fatal attack. The physician also spoke of Nancy's fear of her husband. Others testified regarding their observations in the kitchen and the barn. In light of all the evidence, the jury concluded murder and suicide.

A funeral service for Dyer Pangburn was planned at the North Columbia Church, but the trustees would not allow it. Thus he was simply buried in, most likely, an unmarked grave at the Elizabethtown Cemetery, now called the Spohn Cemetery, on Brewer Road in the town of Columbia. Nancy Sprague was buried next to her first husband at the Dutchtown Cemetery in East Frankfort, leaving her children, her mother and several siblings to mourn her.

MURDER BY THE MANSION

By Mary Haefele

On a winter's night in 1873, Ben Dyckman was on his way home from working in Utica and stopped in Mohawk for a few drinks. He lived south of Mohawk on the Cruger estate, off Robinson Road. His home was a one-and-a-half-story wood house with five rooms downstairs and two upstairs. His mother-in-law, Mrs. Faver, also lived there with him, his wife and their daughter. He also had a lodger, Alfred Travers, living with his family.

Fortified with a few drinks, Ben was determined to make Alfred pay for what he surmised was an unhealthy relationship with his wife. Mrs. Travers occupied the bedroom on the first floor. She heard Ben come home and got up to let him in the back door. She hadn't even gotten back to bed when she heard a commotion in the kitchen. It seems Alfred was upstairs and heard Ben come home and went downstairs to let him in. Before he hit the bottom step someone hit him in the head and dragged him on top of the table. Ben again hit him, this time with the tea kettle. Ben was irate and kept punching him. Alfred pulled out his knife and stabbed Ben.

Hearing all this, Mrs. Faver climbed out her window and started for the neighbor's house. She didn't get very far when Alfred caught up with her and asked if she had talked to anyone. When she replied she had not, Alfred said he would go to their neighbor Joe Mason. Mason was alerted and came to the house to find Ben on the floor with his hands folded. Mrs. Dyckman had come downstairs, and when she saw her husband dead on the floor, she rolled him over and folded his hand across his chest. Another neighbor went to Mohawk and alerted the authorities. Coroner Landt and Dr. Fox came to the Dyckman home. Dr. Fox made a postmortem exam and determined that he had seven knife wounds, with the fatal one penetrating his heart. An exam of Travers revealed that he had bruises on the back of his head with lime sediment around them, apparently from the tea kettle. He had a bruise on his shoulder and hip and a cut over his eye.

Travers was perfectly cool during the inquest. He cut wood, built the fire, carried water and found food to serve the men. Mrs. Dyckman was in a daze, and when she realized what happened, she was heard saying, "Ben, if you would speak to me and tell how this happened I should be satisfied."

This was quite a lot of excitement for the very rural area in which they lived. It must have been the talk of the town. Travers was taken to Herkimer County Jail to await trial. The sheriff sent letters out to see if Alfred was wanted anywhere. When the sheriff of Peekskill opened his mail, he realized that this was the Alfred Dyckman who was wanted for a murder in their area. Alfred had fled the scene, and his cousin Ben Dyckman had taken him in. When Alfred moved to Ben's house, he took his mother's maiden name.

Like Ben, he was a carpenter by trade. In 1868, Alfred was accused of killing Thomas Malloney, an immigrant who got into an argument with Alfred. They were on the docks and were arguing over a voting issue, and Alfred took out a knife and stabbed Malloney. Alfred Dyckman was transferred to Peekskill to stand trial. It was found that the key witness involved had died, so the charges were dropped. Alfred was returned to Herkimer County.

Judge Hardin presided over the court, with District Attorney A.M. Mills the prosecutor and J.A. and A.B. Steele the defendant's lawyers. Mills opened with testimony from the neighbors. Mason described the scene as he found it. Richard Getman testified that the year before, he had heard Alfred say that if Ben didn't stop abusing his wife he would put a stop to it. John Mabbitt of Mohawk said that Ben had a few drinks at his place but that he was not drunk. Next, the defense called several witnesses who attested to the defendant's relationship with his cousin, noting that they were very friendly to each other. The defendant took the stand and described the night in question and said that Ben attacked him and he acted in self-defense. Alfred's elderly mother and sister were in the court room, and it was said they were very distraught. After the closing arguments, Judge Hardin briefly charged the jury, first explaining the law and urged the men to do their whole duty fearlessly. The jury came back with a verdict of murder in the first degree. The prisoner was returned to jail to await sentencing. The judge pronounced the sentence of the law: "That you be taken hence to the place from which you came, to be confined within the common jail of County of Herkimer until the twenty-fifth day of June, 1874, at which time, within the walls of that jail, and between the hours of ten and three o'clock on that day you shall be hanged by the neck until you are dead—and may God have mercy on your soul."

The court adjourned for two weeks to enable counsel to form a writ of error to get a stay of proceedings. On July 23, 1874, the headlines read, "The Dyckman Verdict Reversed—New Trial Ordered." The new trial was short, and no new information was delivered. The retrial resulted in a verdict of murder in the second degree, with a sentence of life in state prison. The prisoner was cool and collected throughout, always asserting his innocence. However, upon returning to jail he became very defiant and disruptive.

Alfred was pardoned on May 14, 1886, from the Auburn prison. The *White Plains Journal* of 1886 noted, "Alfred Dyckman had been in prison for

Gelston Castle. The estate is located off Robinson Road in the town of Warren. Sadly, the castle is in ruins today, with only a few buildings still intact and the family cemetery.

12 years and was pardoned and when released, he wandered about in a daze and could hardly get away from the prison walls."

Alfred died in Peekskill in about 1919. The murder and subsequent trial affected not only the people of Mohawk but also the Dyckman relatives in Peekskill and New York City and the owners of the Cruger mansion.

How did the Dyckmans come to live by the home of Harriet Douglas Cruger, called Henderson House (in later years known as Gelston Castle)? The name Dyckman strikes a familiar chord with Harriet. She would visit her cousin Betsy Corne Dyckman in Westchester County at her Boscobel estate, built by Betsy's husband, Staats Dyckman. Ben and Alfred were both from Westchester County. It may be that they were related to Staats. He was the sixth of nine children, born at his father's inn, the Black Horse Tavern, in Harlem, and had a large extended family. Ben and Alfred were carpenters and were employed on the Cruger estate.

THE MURDERS OF BELLINGER AND HAYES

By Roberta Walsh

It was late on August 4, 1874, and there were only a few people in the saloon in the basement of the building at the corner of Main and Mary Streets in Little Falls, New York. The three customers were Levi Bellinger, James Robinson and a Mr. Rockwell. Charles Reagan was tending bar.

Shortly before 11:00 p.m., Norman Bellinger walked through the saloon door. Reagan could see that he was already under the influence of liquor and told him that the last round was being served because the bar would be closing soon. Norman Bellinger was a horse dealer with a good income, about forty-five years of age and married with one child. He was a drinker but described as a man of peaceful and harmless disposition.

In a separate dining room, Charles Christman was eating oysters when John Roe and Lorenzo Hayes came in and sat down at his table. Roe was a gambler. Lorenzo Hayes was a cooper by trade but had taken up gambling in a small way. Both of them had been drinking before they got there. Roe ordered a lager and would say later that he was so drunk he didn't remember anything that happened that evening.

At about 11:00 p.m. or so, Reagan was closing the bar. The first to leave was Mr. Rockwell, followed by Norman Bellinger a few minutes later, but it took another ten minutes for Reagan to get James Robinson and Levi Bellinger out the saloon door. At more or less the same time, John Moyer was ushering Roe and Hayes out the dining room exit. Christman was already gone.

Within minutes, James Robinson and Levi Bellinger came back to the saloon to tell Reagan and Moyer that there was a man lying outside at the corner of the street. It was so dark they couldn't tell if he was alive or dead. Moyer got a light and went to the street. They found Norman Bellinger lying unconscious and bleeding with a bad cut in back of his right ear. His brother, John, was notified, and Norman was taken home, where Dr. Brainard examined him.

Shortly after Bellinger had been taken home, Hayes returned to Moyer's saloon. Moyer remarked that Norman Bellinger had been attacked and had a pretty ugly wound. Hayes answered, "I did it. He abused me, called me a son of a -----." But, Hayes added, he would go to Bellinger's house in the morning and "make it all right with him." But Bellinger died at about noon on August 5, 1874, without regaining consciousness. Hayes gave himself up to Justice Smith, claiming that he had hit Norman Bellinger in self-defense. Hayes was not locked up, but rather was placed in charge of Officer Roof, who kept him in his house overnight.

At the inquest, the doctors testified that a postmortem examination showed a fractured skull from a single blow from behind with a blunt object, possibly brass knuckles. This injury resulted in a hemorrhage. The coroner's jury returned the verdict that Lorenzo Hayes assaulted Norman Bellinger and that the injury he caused led to Bellinger's death.

Public opinion was squarely against Lorenzo Hayes. He had a reputation for being a rough character and particularly mean when he was drunk. Bellinger, on the other hand, was known to be every bit as good natured when he was drunk as when he was sober. A rumor was going around that Lorenzo Hayes was still nursing a grudge over something that happened in the past when Bellinger was a policeman. What's more, the fact that the killing blow was struck from behind did not support Hayes's story that he attacked Bellinger in self-defense.

Lorenzo Hayes was indicted for the murder of Norman Bellinger in September 1874 and tried at the end of November before Judge George Hardin. He submitted a plea of not guilty but withdrew it, making a deal to plead guilty to manslaughter in the fourth degree. The local paper reported:

> *On Friday last two criminals were sentenced at Herkimer to expiate their offenses, and while the sentences were probably strictly legal in both cases, it will strike the casual observer that either more or less than justice was meted out in one case or the other. Albert Campbell was indicted for grand larceny (stealing), plead guilty, and was sentence to four years, six months imprisonment in Auburn State Prison. Lorenzo Hayes, indicted for murdering a man named Bellinger, at Little Falls, plead guilty of manslaughter in the fourth degree, which plea was accepted and Hayes was sentenced to pay a fine of $250 and be imprisoned one year in the county jail.*

Fifteen years later, on Friday, September 14, 1889, a businessman named F.M. Earl brought two men to the Boyd House Hotel in Mexico, New York, and introduced them to the owner, Captain David Boyd. The two men were Thomas Likens of Potsdam and Lorenzo Hayes of Little Falls. The two men were asking Mr. Earl to build a veneering factory in Herkimer County. Hayes said that they would harvest more than enough timber to supply the factory from the nine thousand acres of timber that he claimed to own there. Likens and Hayes came back the next day to the Boyd House, and after asking the captain to invest in the factory, they were ready for wine and billiards.

Reports of exactly what happened during the rest of the evening differ in the details but agree on the major points. Hayes and Boyd played billiards, and all three man drank for hours. Likens said later that he, Hayes and Boyd consumed more than twenty bottles of wine that afternoon and evening. Shortly after 11:00 p.m., Boyd tried to close down and convince Hayes and Likens to go to their rooms, but Hayes refused to quit playing. Finally, the men were told that the bar was out of wine. When Hayes got angry, Boyd

Boyd House, Main Street, Mexico, New York, in the 1920s. The general appearance of the building didn't change much from the 1880s.

told the bartender to go down to the cellar and get another bottle. Hayes swore at the bartender. Boyd made a remark to him, and Hayes turned on Boyd and knocked him to the floor. As Hayes grabbed Boyd around the neck and started to choke him, Mrs. Boyd yelled for the bartender to call the constable. Hayes, younger and a much bigger man, had the advantage on Boyd. On the floor with Hayes holding him down, Boyd stabbed wildly at Hayes with his pocketknife before passing out. With Mrs. Boyd screaming and the constable on his way, Hayes ran up the stairs and locked himself in a room, where a Dr. Bennett saw him later.

After he sobered up, Hayes made a deal with Boyd that, in exchange for $300, he would not hold Boyd responsible for stabbing him. He had as many as thirteen cuts, but they had been made with a small knife and appeared to be superficial. The longest, about two and a half inches, was across the side of his face.

The following Thursday, Hayes went back to Little Falls. He soon came down with a fever. The cut on his face had obviously become infected, and Hayes died a week later. Everyone concerned with the incident was very surprised when news reached Oswego that Hayes had died. The second surprise came when they found out that after returning to Little Falls, Hayes signed a witnessed statement saying that he did nothing to provoke Boyd and that he only attacked Boyd when he was forced to do so in self-defense.

In Oswego, District Attorney Stowell swore out a warrant of murder in the first degree for David Boyd. Later, after learning the circumstances of the fight, he asked the grand jury to change the charge to manslaughter in the first degree. Boyd was indicted, pleaded not guilty and was released on $6,000 bail.

Captain Boyd's trial for manslaughter started on the last Monday in January 1889 and lasted about eight days. The prosecution was conducted by Assistant District Attorney Clark and Mr. Mead of Fulton. Colonel W.G. Robinson of Oswego and C.C. Brown of Mexico conducted the defense. The jury was out for two hours, and at the end of that time, Captain Boyd was pronounced not guilty. There was applause in the courtroom.

THE MURDER OF ORLO DAVIS

By Roberta Walsh

On Thursday, June 23, 1875, Albert Fredenburg went out to milk the cows and, on his way back to the house, stopped at the barn to look for eggs. Inside he found his uncle, Orlo, lying dead; he said later that he supposed Orlo had committed suicide. Albert sent word to Captain William S. Burt, the justice of the peace at Grayville.

Life had been hard for Orlo Davis. Sometime earlier, Orlo had deeded his farm to his son, Franklin. This was done on condition that his son would allow him to remain in the house and would provide for him for the rest of his life. But once Franklin had taken over the farm, the family made Orlo work for his keep, locking him outdoors for hours chopping wood and doing other chores. Next, the family kicked him out of the house completely and moved his bed out to the barn. This may not have been as bad as it sounds, as neighbors claimed that the barn was cleaner than the house. In the early spring, Franklin had tried to get rid of his father altogether by putting him in the county poorhouse, but it had refused to take him on the grounds that he had a home and a family who were able to take care of him.

Orlo suffered from St. Anthony's dance, a disease that causes, among other things, uncoordinated jerking movements of the face, hands and feet. To make matters worse, his hands got frostbitten from working outdoors, and nerve damage made them virtually useless.

When Captain Burt arrived at the Davis farm, it didn't take him long to realize that he was looking at a murder. Orlo Davis had been almost completely decapitated. A huge gash on the left side of his neck had separated his jawbone from the rest of his face and severed his spine and spinal cord, cutting both his jugular vein and carotid artery. He must have died immediately. And there was no sign of a weapon anywhere around the body. The axe that did the job was found inside the house.

Coroner Hamlin was notified and immediately began to make arrangements for a coroner's jury to meet in Middleville. Drs. Hamlin, Hall and Streeter made a postmortem of the body. In those days before television, the old armory building was barely large enough to hold the number of people who wanted to attend the inquest to hear the evidence and see the bloody axe.

Sheriff Eaton and Deputy Snyder were at the inquest, holding the suspects under arrest. There were six: Almira Underwood Davis, age fifty-four, wife of the victim; Lodicia Underwood Fredenburg, age sixty-eight, Almira's older sister; Albert Fredenburg, age thirty-seven, son of Lodicia; Franklin Davis, age twenty-one, son of Orlo Davis; Mary Fredenburg Davis, age sixteen, newlywed wife of Franklin Davis (daughter of Albert Fredenburg and granddaughter of Lodicia); and George Adams, who lived on the neighboring farm. Captain Burt and others involved with the investigation gave evidence, and members of the family were questioned. When Mary was called, the newspapers reported that "she testified like all the others of the clan, evidently knowing more than she cared to tell, and telling some things that she didn't know."

Reporters described the prime suspect for those who were not able to attend. "Old Mrs. Fredenburg is a character," they said. "She is of medium height and weighs about two hundred pounds. Her head is small, eyes sharp and black, and her tongue runs as glibly as a telegraph machine. Her head sits closely upon her shoulders and looks like a hand ball on the top of a beer pitcher." Lodicia Fredenburg was charged with murder and Albert Fredenburg, Franklin Davis and Mary Davis with being accomplices. Almira Davis and George Adams were released.

In November 1875, Judge Milton H. Merwin presided over the "Gray Murder Trial" in a crowded courtroom. The Fredenburgs were defended by Sewell S. Morgan, while Mary and Franklin Davis were represented by George W. Smith. Mary and Franklin gave state's evidence, which eventually led to them being discharged from custody. Mary testified that Lodicia and Albert had plotted to kill Orlo, and in the middle of the night on June 23, they had threatened her to make her carry the lantern for them. She was nine months' pregnant at the time. She testified that Albert had carried the axe to the barn but that Lodicia had actually struck the killing blow. Lodicia and Albert Fredenburg were both found guilty of murder in the first degree. The sentence pronounced by the court was that the prisoners be returned to the jail and that, on Friday, December 31, between the hours of 10:00 a.m. and 4:00 p.m., they be hanged by the neck until dead.

Albert was understandably dismayed at Mary's testimony and wrote out a statement to be published after his death. It said, in part, "[W]hen I got hom it was ten buy my clock I then eate my super and Went to bed and did Not git up til morning and did Not have eney talk With eney one a boute killing orlo Davis nor Did not kill him nor did not know he Was a gouing to be kild nor Did not See him kild and did not know he Was kild till I Went in to the barn the next morning to get Some eggs and found him Ded I am as Inesent as a child unborne of the killing of Orlo Davis."

In the middle of December, with only two weeks before the death sentence was to be carried out, Mary confessed that her testimony at the trial was false and that she alone had gone with Lodicia to the barn to kill Orlo—Albert had nothing to do with it. As a result of this, and due to a petition by Albert's lawyer, a delay was granted by Governor Tilden to give counsel an opportunity to apply for a new trial. After the judge turned down the request for a new trial, the governor commuted Albert's death sentence to life in prison. Governor Tilden was quoted as saying, "[I] would not hang a dog on such testimony."

Lodicia's sentence was commuted to life in prison based on her age and evidence that she was not mentally stable. She was imprisoned in the hospital wing at Sing Sing until November 1877, when the female convicts were transferred from Sing Sing to the Kings County Penitentiary in Brooklyn. She died there on July 18, 1884.

Kings County Penitentiary in Brooklyn, where Lodicia Fredenburg died in 1884.

Albert Fredenburg was sent to Auburn. In 1903, Governor Odell was petitioned by friends on Albert's behalf to commute his sentence to time served: twenty-seven years, one month and sixteen days. Albert went home to Gray and died of consumption six weeks later on October 13, 1903.

Franklin Davis had been released from jail in May 1876, and Mary Davis was released one month later once the authorities had determined that they were no longer needed as witnesses.

Almira Davis, widow of Orlo Davis, died at the county poorhouse in March 1876 and was buried at Norway—at least for a while. In May, a woman's arm and leg were found in the apartment of a medical student. Newspapers reported that Almira Davis's body had been dug up, cut up and salted down, but the people responsible for it apparently escaped punishment.

THE MURDER OF MOSES CRAIG HOLDEN SR.

By Susan Perkins

Moses Craig Holden Sr. of Herkimer was a fifty-year-old blacksmith who had married Julia Lampman on August 27, 1849. They had two daughters, Viola and Lillian. His murderer, Alphonso Klock of Jacksonburg, was nineteen years old, the son of Ira and Catherine (Staring) Klock. The cause of the murder was on account of Holden's intimacy with Alphonso's sister, Mary. Mary was twenty-four years old and had had a baby girl born on January 8, 1880. Moses Holden was the father.

Holden and Mary became acquainted while they were employed on the farm of J.C. Tower in the eastern part of the town of Little Falls before they ran away in 1878 to Syracuse, where people assumed they were married. Alphonso Klock and William Casler (brother-in-law married to Libbie C. Klock) learned of Mary's whereabouts. They went to Syracuse to bring her home. Holden was arrested for bastardy and was held in the Herkimer County Jail. He was later released.

On Sunday, August 8, 1880, Holden learned that Mary was working for a distant relative, Elias Klock, living in the town of Little Falls on the Herkimer side of the Mohawk River. According to Mary's story, Holden arrived on the premises at about eleven o'clock that night. He blew a whistle, to which she responded. She met him at the fence, and they talked for a few minutes.

Then they went to the cow barn, where they were discovered by her brother, Alphonso, who had heard Mary scream. Alphonso shot Holden in the left breast, severing an artery leading to the heart. Holden had been warned by Mary's family against going to see Mary, as members of the family had threatened to shoot him.

Alphonso gave himself up after he had hired counsel Mills, Palmer & Morgan. He was brought to Herkimer on August 9, 1880, and put in jail to await his fate. According to the *Herkimer Democrat*, "The affair has created considerable excitement, and but little sympathy is expressed for either the deceased or his murderer."

The paper went on to report, "Mary Klock, the direct cause of the tragedy, was the first witness called. She is a very fair woman of 24, with dark eyes, black hair, fair complexion….While Mary appeared to be of ordinary intelligence she developed an apparent lack of realization of the serious character of the investigation, and frequently rounded out her replies to the coroner's questions with a laugh. District Attorney Steele, Jurors Mc Crone and Nau and others took turns in petting the baby and trying to keep it quiet. This gave Mary considerable amusement, as she seemed proud of the child, paying more attention to that than to the inquest." In her testimony, she did confirm that Holden took liberties in the barn.

Moses Holden's widow, Julia Holden, testified at the trial that she had not lived with Moses for more than two years. They had been separated before. He was immoral and in every way unfaithful to his family. She worked very hard to take care of the family because he did not work. She was a seamstress. She also stated that he drank for fifteen years and that they were only happy for two years of their marriage. Holden had served in the 152nd Infantry during the Civil War. She felt that he pretended he was sick so he could come home from the war. Holden claimed he had found religion. They then moved to Michigan with $1,000. He hadn't changed his ways and got into trouble while living there. The family then moved back to Herkimer. Julia kept taking back her husband but finally was ready to file for divorce, at which time he got angry and stormed out of the house. Julia made the following statement: "It was not until sometime after that I heard of his relations with her. I went to see the girl in June last, and had a plain talk with her. She is not a bright girl. She said she did not wish to have anything more to do with Holden and I thought she was sincere in what she said. She seemed to be entirely rid of her infatuation for the man. I considered it my duty to go and talk with her, as I wanted to do anything I could to prevent further scandal, for the sake of my children."

Alphonso was sentenced on February18, 1881. He was found guilty of third-degree manslaughter and sentenced to two years' imprisonment at the Auburn prison. He was released on October 10, 1884.

Mary Klock is listed in the 1880 census as living with her parents in the town of Little Falls. Her child is not listed in the household. A mystery remains in what happened to Mary: she disappeared without a trace. In the 1892 census in Little Falls, there is a Mary Klock, age sixty-two; Robert, age forty; Jacob, age twenty-four; and a girl named Etta May, age twelve. Could Etta May be Mary's daughter?

The Casler, Klock and Staring genealogies do not tell what happened to Mary Klock. They do not even mention Etta May Klock.

THE JOHN WISHART MURDER

By Barbara Dunadee

John Wishart, at seventy-one years old, was a longtime Schuyler resident, having emigrated from Germany as a young man. Viewed by his family as cantankerous and opinionated, John was often referred to as "the old man" by his wife, Nancy, fourteen years his junior and the thirteen Wishart children, several of whom were teenagers still living at home. While John could read and write, neither his wife nor the majority of his children were able to do so. A man of meager means, John was employed as a farmworker on land owned by Sanford Getman, located on the Central Depot in Ilion (present-day River Street).

John Wishart was last seen alive on April 17, 1884. He was spotted buying a sack of flour from Lints Grocery in Frankfort. It was his intention to give the flour to his daughter-in-law so that she could make him a loaf of bread.

Earlier that month, John had become homeless after being angrily kicked out of his Schuyler home by his wife. The conflict between them and other family members had been brewing ever since the fall of 1883, when twenty-six-year-old Frank Mondon, an Italian immigrant and West Shore Line railroad worker, began courting his fourteen-year-old daughter Loesa. John's dislike for the four-foot-eleven, dark-haired Mondon intensified when rumors spread that he had a wife and child in Italy. Nancy Wishart did not share her husband's negative view of Mondon, instead encouraging his and Loesa's relationship. Ignoring her father's protests, Loesa married Mondon in February. The couple took up residence in John's house, to John's dismay. John voiced his frustration over the marriage, and heated outbursts ensued. The home became a war zone, with lines drawn between John on one side and the others who lived with him on the other. He was physically ousted, and the door was barred by his teenage son Frederick at Nancy Wishart's urging. Unable to enter his own home, John stayed instead with his son Adam and his wife, Hattie, in their nearby residence. However, the hostilities continued, and John's eviction appeared to be permanent.

One evening, when his father did not show up at his house, Adam did not worry. He had assumed that his father had traveled to see Adam's brother in Syracuse, as he had been planning. Days and then weeks went by, and the elder Wishart had not returned. Adam contacted his brother in Syracuse, only to learn that his father had never made the journey. He began a frantic search for his father.

The next sighting of John Wishart, this time as a decomposing corpse, came on May 8, 1884, when Adam discovered his father's body on the Getman farm in Ilion, lying facedown among the rocks in the soggy bottom of a steep ditch that ran from the river to the railroad. Adam recognized his father by his pants and boots. He ran to the nearby farmhouse to get help. Mr. Getman and Adam descended into the ditch. Before Adam turned his father over, Mr. Getman advised him that the coroner from Ilion needed to be contacted.

Once Coroner Robert Warner arrived, the body was examined. It was apparent that a brutal attack had taken place. A broken piece of driftwood, wide enough to be used as a club, was found nearby. The body and the club were taken back to the village for further examination by medical personnel. Deputy Sheriff Delos W. Finster and Constable A. Frank Clark of Frankfort began investigating the death.

What followed was a chain of criminal proceedings that stretched out over two and a half years, during which it would be determined how John Wishart had died and who would be held responsible. First a coroner's inquest took place in May at which physicians Parkhurst, Budlong and Lehr began by stating that John had received a heavy blow from the back, fracturing his skull, breaking the left parietal and temporal lobes and bones of the nose. This injury was enough to have caused death, but the victim may have lingered an hour or more before succumbing. Other cuts and bruises on the body may have come when John fell down the embankment.

As for motive, investigators focused on John's volatile relationship with his family. Verbal threats had been made to him by several members, including his wife, his youngest daughter and, in particular, his son-in-law, Frank Mondon.

He was the person who had imbedded himself into John's household, usurping John's authority and position. Mondon, who spoke little English, had been quoted as repeatedly condemning the man, saying, "I will fix him in one lick." Mondon was charged with premeditated murder. The dead man's wife, Nancy, was indicted as an accessory. A grand jury held in November came to the same conclusion as the coroner's inquest. Former district attorney J.J. Duggleston Jr. and attorney H. Clay Hall were appointed to defend Mondon.

The trial was convened by Fifth District New York State Supreme Court justice Pardon C. Williams (1842–1925) on Thursday, May 21, 1885. The jury listened as District Attorney Abram Steele and W.C. Prescott opened the proceedings by presenting a map of the area where the victim was found and photographs of the body. The devastating injuries were once again described. Potential weapons were identified by Dr. A. Walter Suiter. Neighbors told of overhearing raucous arguments coming from the Wishart residence. Witnesses testified, repeating Mondon's threats against John. A confused Loesa Wishart Mondon, who at first said she did not know the defendant, recanted and said that her husband had confessed to her that he had killed her father, having warned her not to tell anyone or else he would kill her.

Sheriff Valentine Brown was questioned about finding a trunk in Mondon's possession containing John Wishart's knife and pocketbook. The sheriff also described a discussion he had with Mondon while the prisoner was in incarceration. Mondon told him that he witnessed Adam Wishart striking his father with a stick and throwing his father's lifeless body into a ditch. Adam's wife, Hattie, and his sister Julia Couch refuted Mondon's jailhouse claims, swearing that Adam was with them fishing at the time in question. The prosecution rested its case after three days.

The defense called no witnesses and presented no evidence on Mondon's behalf. However, in his closing arguments, defense attorney Hall spoke for two and a half hours, picking apart the state's case. Then D.A. Steele summarized the prosecution's arguments for conviction. The jury deliberated for several hours and came back with a verdict of murder in the first degree.

On Tuesday, May 26, 1885, Judge Williams ordered that the convicted murderer's execution by hanging take place on Friday, July 10, 1885, in Herkimer. Mondon's lawyers appealed the decision, delaying the execution, and eventually obtained a new trial, set to begin on December 3, 1886. A plea deal was reached shortly before the second trial was to start. Frank Mondon pleaded guilty to murder in the second degree, avoiding death. Judge Williams resentenced him to life imprisonment.

Mondon arrived at the Auburn prison on December 7, 1886, where he remained until January 1892. At this time, he was transferred to an asylum for the criminally insane. He remained institutionalized as an insane convict until his death in 1926 at Dannemora State Hospital at age sixty-eight.

Nancy Wishart's accessory charges were dropped. She lived into her mid-eighties, residing with her son Frederick in Schuyler. In his will, John left his property to his daughter Antinette, with no mention of his wife. John and Nancy are buried at the East Schuyler Miller Cemetery.

The cemetery stone for John Wishart, spelled "Wisherd" on the stone.

A TIMELESS TRAGEDY

By Fran Peruzzi

Eugenia (Jennie) Ball was born in 1858. She, along with her parents and two sisters, emigrated from England to the United States and resided in Ilion. When her mother died, Jennie and her sister Belle were adopted by David and Matilda DeVoe. The DeVoes were wealthy and lived in a plush house in Ilion. Jennie became very accomplished as a musician and sang at the Ilion Methodist Church. She was described as having a radiant personality and was liked by all.

Thomas Parkes worked at the Ilion Remington Manufacturing Company in the office as a bookkeeper. Jennie and Thomas married on September 27, 1875. For several years, they lived in the DeVoe house, and in April 1882, they moved to their own house on Prospect Street in Herkimer.

Sometime before moving to Herkimer, Thomas, in partnership with his longtime friend Mr. Barry, started a business located in Herkimer. The Parkes, Barry & Company store was a drug and grocery enterprise. The store had several employees, including a bookkeeper.

Jennie and Thomas's union was blessed with two daughters. Lulu was five years old in March 1883, and their newborn was just eight weeks old. To everyone, even their live-in servant, Delia Bly, they appeared to be a happy couple, but there were ongoing rumors that Thomas was not faithful to Jennie. The rumors and talk of family ill treatment and infidelity by Thomas were persistent. Later, during an official inquest by Dr. A. Walter Suiter, Thomas addressed some of the rumors. One rumor was in regard to Alice Day, an Ilion woman. He denied being the father of Alice's child. Thomas further stated there were no improper relations with his store bookkeeper and general clerk Miss Grace Riley. Thomas said that he spoke to his wife, Jennie, about the rumors for several hours during October 1882. Thomas noted that he dispelled the rumors to his wife's satisfaction. He also dispelled some of the rumors during the inquest.

According to testimony at the inquest given by Thomas Parkes and the domestic servant, Delia Bly, March 25, 1883, seemed like a typical Sunday for the Parkes family. They arose, had breakfast and settled into their Sunday routine. Jennie asked Thomas to play the piano while she sang. Later, Thomas went to church and afterward walked to the store. Then he met two other men and had a cigar with them at the hotel. Thomas then returned to the store to fill a medical order for one of the men who had a sick family member. He returned home with a headache, which he said was common. Thomas and Jennie read a Shakespeare play, which Thomas finished while lying down. Jennie came and lay down with him. She put the baby in his arms, and the baby cooed as she only did for him. Jennie wished to go out. Thomas dozed until she returned around seven o'clock. Thomas then went out to check the fires at the store. (In 1883, gas and electricity were just starting to be used in street lighting and industry and was not readily used in residences and small businesses.) It should be noted that according to newspaper reports at the time, Thomas generally went out every night and did not return until ten or eleven o'clock or later. Before leaving, Thomas related how Jennie asked Lulu, their daughter, to get ready for bed. When she did not do as told, Thomas then asked her to get ready for bed. When Lulu still did not do as told, Thomas struck her twice on the ears. According to Thomas, Jennie "remonstrated him for his treatment of the child." He told Jennie to not "interfere when I am correcting my child." Thomas claimed that was "the harshest thing I ever said to Jennie."[12] Thomas left the house and could not be located until eleven o'clock.

Shortly before eight o'clock that evening, Jennie asked the servant to go next door and ask Mrs. Bull to come over. This was a normal request from Jennie. Upon returning with Mrs. Bull, they met with a horrible discovery.

UTICA, SATURDAY, MARCH 31, 1883.

MRS. THOMAS PARKES of Herkimer.
WHO SHOT HER TWO CHILDREN, SUNDAY, AND THEN HERSELF.

HERKIMER'S TRAGEDY.

3-31-1883

MRS. THOMAS PARKES' AWFUL DEED.

[illegible] Her Two Children and

MRS. PARKES.

Deceased was not quite 25 years old, and bore an estimable reputation in the community. She was born in England and named Eugenie Ball. The family came to this country and settled in Ilion while deceased was yet a child. She was adopted into the family of David D. Devoe, of that village. She was married to her husband

Clipping from a Utica newspaper.

Jennie lay in bed between her two children. She had shot each child in the head and then herself. Jennie was dead. The children lived for several hours before dying. The pistol was still grasped in Jennie's right hand. It was never discovered when and how Jennie obtained the pistol.

One will never know Jennie's view of the family environment. Rumors of Thomas's infidelity and his ill treatment of family were persistent and

Gravestone of Eugenia and her two children at Oak Hill Cemetery in Herkimer.

ongoing. Neighbors, friends and the servant indicated that Jennie never said anything to them. Outwardly, it seemed to be a happy family. Was there ill treatment and infidelity? The March 28, 1883 *Rome Daily Sentinel*, quoting the *Utica Herald*, expressed what some people were thinking: "Mr. Parkes, in his evidence, settled one scandal, but did not tell why he was in the habit of remaining away from the home almost every evening until 10 or 11 and sometimes 12 o'clock, nor why he was in the company of a single lady for three hours on Sunday evening while his wife was home alone. In staying away as he did, he only increased the suspicion that was lurking in the bosom of his wife."[13]

That Sunday evening, Thomas did go to the store and then visited Miss Grace Riley, his bookkeeper, at her residence in Herkimer for about three hours. During the coroner's inquest, Thomas vaguely alluded to trying to train Miss Riley in a bookkeeping double-entry system. Thomas learned about the tragedy when he left Miss Riley's residence and went to the home of his friend Mr. Barry.

The coroner's inquest concluded that no one else was to blame, including Thomas Parkes. A physician explained that Jennie had puerperal mania (what is presently known as postpartum depression), which may have contributed to a state of temporary insanity leading to her tragic actions. Newspapers at the time suggested that the prevalent and persistent rumors of infidelity may have exacerbated Jennie's mental state to a tragic point. During the inquest, it was mentioned that some of Thomas's relatives advised Thomas to move from the area.

The funeral took place on March 28, 1883, in the afternoon at the Ilion Methodist Church. In a beautiful white casket, Jennie had the baby in her arms. Lulu looked like she was sleeping nearby in her own casket. The church was completely filled with people. A crowd also gathered outside to pay their respects. For forty-five minutes, mourners filed by the caskets. Jennie and her two children share the same grave, side by side, at the Herkimer Oak Hill Cemetery.

What happened to Thomas Parkes? He did move from the area. Thomas remarried a little more than a year later on April 26, 1884, to Grace Riley in Springfield, Massachusetts. With his second wife, they had three boys and lived in Manhattan. Thomas became a successful proprietor of two hotels, the Grand View in Lake Placid, New York, and the Hargrave Hotel in New York City. Thomas and his second wife are buried at the North Elba Cemetery in Lake Placid.

THE HANGING OF A MURDERESS

By Richard G. Case

The crime that brought Roxalana Druse to the gallows in Herkimer took place on the Druse farm in Warren on December 18, 1884, the Thursday before Christmas. It did not come to general notice for nearly three weeks.

Roxalana and William Druse and their children, Mary and George, lived in a small house with a green door on the spine of a hill on what now is Chyle Road. The Druses farmed about ninety acres; the place had a worn-out look about it even then. "It is a hard looking place for the abode of man," a Utica newspaper reporter wrote.

William Druse was fifty-six at the time of his death. George was nine and Mary nineteen. The family was in debt and had a poor reputation in the neighborhood, especially William. Testimony at the trial portrayed him as a lazy oddball who had a bad temper. He wore a long beard, tinkered with inventions and like to read magazines and newspapers. He visited neighbors and stayed for hours, talking to no one.

His wife claimed that he beat her. Mrs. Druse came from Sangerfield. She was forty-two. She met her husband when she came to Warren to pick hops. They had been married twenty years when she killed him. In an interview with a reporter a few days before she died, Mrs. Druse said it probably would have been best not to marry William. She thought they were mismatched.

Roxalana's sister, Lucy, lived with her husband, Charles Gates, and four children half a mile west of the Druse farm. One of her sons also was charged as an accomplice in the crime. Frank Gates was fourteen. He was staying with the Druses to help with farm work. Frank said he was first up that morning. He helped George and his father do the chores, while Mary

William and Roxalana Druse.

and Mrs. Druse got breakfast. There was an argument during the meal. George heard his father threaten to kill his mother.

George described the scene when he testified at his mother's trial: "He went to blowing Ma; he swore at her.…Ma told us to get out around the corner of the house; we went out there and then we heard a revolver go off. Then Ma called Frank. She told him to shoot; he shot.…[Later] Ma went out and got the axe and the head was cut off; she cut off the head from father."

The son said he saw the head wrapped in a shirt and put in the parlor. The rest of the body was on a high straw tick. He said he wasn't sure what happened after that.

The prosecutor contended that Mrs. Druse tried to burn the body in the parlor stove. Neighbors recalled seeing acrid, black smoke coming from the chimney. When inquiries were made about the missing man, Mrs. Druse said he had gone to New York City.

A cornerstone of the people's case that there had, indeed, been a murder and that a body existed to prove it was provided by Dr. A. Walter Suiter of Herkimer. The physician (a pioneer in forensic medicine) was hired by District Attorney Abram Steele to make a detailed scientific study of the remains and decide if the bone fragments found by investigators at the farm were human.

The Druse kitchen, the scene of the crime. *Courtesy of Richfield Springs Historical Society.*

Yes, he testified, a number of the fragments were human. He produced a floorboard from the house. It was stained with human blood. Suiter's courtroom appearance—he brought microscope slides with him to show the bone fragments he picked from the "chaotic mass" he found at the farm—hardly suggested the depth of the investigation. It was a fine piece of medical detective work. The doctor himself later described his study for the Druse case as "quite unparalleled in the history of crime."

Roxalana's lawyer argued justifiable homicide at her trial. DeWight Luce opened the defense on September 30, 1885, to an overflow crowd in the courtroom. Two-thirds of the spectators that day were women. He said that William Druse had attempted to kill his wife with an axe and she shot at him during the struggle. The head was removed in a frenzy, he said.

The major witness for the defense was Mary Druse, Roxalana's daughter. Luce led her through a recital of ill-treatment her mother received from her father. Once, she said, he hit her with a horsewhip and then gave a neighbor five dollars to keep quiet about the incident.

The morning of the murder, Mary said that William yelled at his wife about cutting up a board and then threatened to "split her brains" with an axe. At breakfast, he complained about the tea and struck Roxalana in the face with his fist. Then he took a knife from the table and told her he was about to cut her throat. It was at that point, according to Mary, that the first shot was fired.

Judge Pardon Williams's charge to the jury of twelve farmers and businessmen took note of the serious controversy in the case—not that William had been killed but whether the act was "justifiable or excusable." He said he did not believe the dead man's disposition and cruelty were legal justifications for murder. Rather, he said, the jurors had to decide if Mrs. Druse was in "some great personal danger."

The jury deliberated slightly more than five hours before finding Mrs. Druse guilty of murder in the first degree. Sentence was passed two days later. The judge ordered Mrs. Druse hanged "by and under the direction of Herkimer County by the neck until you be dead" on November 25, 1885.

The first hanging date was not kept. A respite of sentence was granted by the governor's office during October because an appeal had been filed. Mrs. Druse passed the first anniversary of the murder in her cell.

The next July, Mrs. Druse and her lawyer appeared before a judge in Utica, and Luce argued his appeal. He admitted his client's greatest mistake was to try to conceal the body by burning it. Mrs. Druse, when asked by the judge, said she didn't think she had a fair trial. The judge, George Hardin, decided the trial had been fair, legal and correct. He resentenced Mrs. Druse to be executed on August 19, 1886.

There was another respite. Luce filed an appeal of Hardin's judgement with the New York Court of Appeals. The decision did not appear until October 26. The judges concurred with the lower court; they saw no reason for disturbing the verdict. This set the stage for a new resentencing ritual by Judge Williams in Herkimer. It took place on November 8. Mrs. Druse stood in front of the justice in a black suit, her eyes on the floor and appearing to a reporter "pale and emaciated."

She was to be hanged four days after Christmas. Now only the governor or an act of the legislature could save her from the gallows. Legislators could amend the state penal code to exempt women from the death penalty in capital cases. Such a bill was introduced during January, but it died in the Judiciary Committee.

In these final weeks, the case attracted the interest of other members of the clergy, women's rights organizations, temperance groups and advocates of abolishing capital punishment. Feminists declared Roxy to be a victim of a male-dominated society where women lacked the vote and therefore couldn't control their own destinies. Letters and petitions about the case began to arrive at the governor's office in early November 1886, asking the governor to commute her sentence. The governor took no more action. He sided with the law, saying that he found no grounds for executive clemency. He had sent a team of medical experts to the jail to verify Mrs. Druse's sanity. And he asked Judge Williams for his opinion. A criminal's gender shouldn't make a difference, Williams said.

The new execution date was to be February 28. This time the sentence was carried out. The scaffold used to carry out the court's sentence had been built at Fort Plain for the hanging of Charles Eacker at Fonda in 1871. It was constructed so it could be dismantled, stored, moved and erected again. Sheriff Cook ordered it painted glossy white and striped black.

Public hangings were outlawed in New York State in 1835. The law put them in closed jail yards and limited the number of witnesses. Twelve "citizens of Herkimer County" were listed officially as witnesses. The number probably was higher, including a member of the press who was allowed to watch from a window in the jail attic.

February 28, 1887, cleared from a blizzard the day before. It was a Monday. The sheriff ordered out the local militia unit, the Remington Rifles of Mohawk, to keep order among those who gathered outside the jail that day. The village was crowded. At 10:00 a.m., the militia marched from the depot to the courthouse to the slow, steady, soft cadence of a drum. Roxalana wore a black satin dress to the gallows. It was the same one she had on at her trial. At the top of her bodice, there was a bunch of roses from a large bouquet Mary had sent to her.

The gallows stood on the ground, near the Court Street gate and almost under the prisoner's window. The execution party moved into the yard at 11:30 a.m. Sheriff Cook and Undersheriff A.M. Rice were in front of Roxalana and Reverend Powell. She held the minister's arm. Roxalana and her minister knelt on the plank floor of the scaffold and prayed. Then Powell spoke for her. He said she asked her enemies to forgive her, since she forgave everyone.

Two special deputies adjusted straps around the prisoner's arm and drew a black cap across her face. When the noose was slipped over her head, she cried out, "Oh, dear!" Then she let go with a "piteous wail." The sheriff gave the signal to spring the trap that held the iron counterweight in place. Her body leaped into the air, and the handkerchief she had been holding fluttered to the ground.

Two doctors, Walter Suiter and Cyrus Kay, declared that Roxalana had died of asphyxiation. They said she was unconscious as soon as the noose tightened. The body remained suspended from the noose for about fifteen minutes before it was lowered onto the bier. That was when the witnesses were called up to look at the corpse. Someone noticed that the rope had crushed the roses at her throat.

Roxalana was placed in an unmarked grave at Oak Hill Cemetery on the hillside west of Herkimer.

MURDER IN MIDDLEVILLE

By Jane Dieffenbacher

In 1885, Middleville was a bustling community. A trip to Herkimer took forty minutes on the Herkimer, Newport and Poland narrow-gauge railway. News traveled quickly, and Middleville people discussed the January arrest of Roxalana Druse and a few other murders that had taken place in the Mohawk Valley towns in 1884. But of course, nothing of that sort ever happened in peaceful Middleville.

On February 28, 1885, shots were fired from a revolver that resulted in the death of one man, the ruin of another man and considerable excitement in Middleville. A man lay dead in the snow in front of a doctor's house on the corner of what is now called Fairfield Street and Reservoir Road.

The story begins in Germany, where Moritz Richter was born in 1825. After receiving a medical education at the University of Leipzig, Dr. Richter came to the United States in 1854. He became naturalized in 1859 and found his way to Middleville, where he purchased a home in which he built his medical practice and was known to the locals as the "Dutch doctor."

In 1876, at the age of fifty-one, Dr. Richter married thirty-six-year-old Eliza Ward, daughter of farmer Sidney Ward, who lived on the road to Little Falls in Eatonville. It was said at the time that Mr. Ward was surprised and dismayed by the marriage. However, Eliza assumed the role of doctor's wife and lived an apparently happy life until February 1884, when the doctor returned her to her father's house. It was said that he regarded her as "partially insane," as she was acting strangely. She left her clothing and belongings in the doctor's house. At this time, she also held two mortgages on this house, assigned to her by her father, who had obtained them from a friend of the doctor.

The victim of this murder case was Professor Syrus Clark Smith, born in 1858, son of Herkimer farmer Hubbard H. Smith. At the age of eighteen, he entered Fairfield Seminary. Later, he taught in local district schools and served as principal of the Salisbury Union School for three years. In 1884, he left Salisbury for a position in Fairfield Seminary and taught at the Fairfield Village District School no. 6 at the same time. His wife was Mary Getman, whom he married in 1879.

Dr. Moritz Richter.

How did the paths of the Dutch doctor and the Fairfield teacher intersect resulting in murder? Mary Getman Smith and Malvin Getman, her brother, were parties in a land transfer of the Sidney Ward farm to Eliza Richter and others in 1885. A relationship apparently existed between the Wards and Getmans.

Divorce being extremely rare in the 1880s, Eliza Richter continued living on her father's farm. She sold her personal effects that were left in the Richter home to S. Clark Smith for $200 about one year followed her removal to the farm.

On the morning of February 28, 1885, S. Clark Smith and his brother-in-law, Malvin Getman, visited Dr. Richter with the bill of sale. The doctor put his wife's clothing, jewelry and mink furs into a trunk and boxes that they carried downstairs and placed in the sleigh. The doctor said that he wanted to consult his counsel before releasing some furniture.

At about 4:30 p.m., Smith visited Charles W. Taber, a Fairfield constable who resided in Middleville, and showed him papers regarding the release of furniture in the doctor's house. The constable accompanied Smith to the doctor's house, where they were admitted and served the doctor with the papers. In dismay, the doctor said the chamber set was upstairs. Charles Taber went up to get it, followed by Smith. When Taber turned around, he saw the doctor fire his revolver at Smith. Smith ran past the doctor and down the stairs crying, "Oh my God"; he continued out the front door and fell in the snow.

Two shots had been fired, and the constable testified that the revolver was then pointed at him. He seized the revolver from the doctor's hand and led

SCENE OF THE LATE MIDDLEVILLE TRAGEDY.

him downstairs. He helped him put on his coat, tied his arms with a strap from the barn and took him to the justice's office.

Middleville was in a high state of excitement. Coroner Dr. A.J. Browne of Newport had empaneled a jury, and the inquest proceeded immediately. Meanwhile, Dr. Richter was taken to the county jail at Herkimer.

At the inquest, it was revealed that the .38-caliber revolver held four bullets, two of which were fired at Smith. Each shot could have caused death, the second one having passed through the heart. On April 16, 1885, the grand jury indicted Roxalana Druse for the murder of her husband and Dr. Richter for murder in the first degree of S. Clark Smith. On April 17, they were both arraigned, and both pleaded not guilty.

Dr. Richter's trial began on October 6, with District Attorney Abram B. Steele and William C. Prescott appearing for the people and George W. Smith and J.A. Steele for the defense. At the trial, it was revealed that Dr. Richter had treated patients up to and including the day of the shooting. Lydia Wood testified that she was in the office for some medicine and that the doctor appeared excited, pacing the floor. Finally, the doctor cried several times while telling her of his troubles. He told her of Smith's first visit of the day and said that Smith was capable of hurting his feelings more than any person he knew.

Dr. Theodore Deecke of the State Lunatic Asylum at Utica testified that he found Dr. Richter to be suffering from a "chronic disease of the spine called locomotor ataxia." The functional capacity of the brain would be thereby affected.

After the final arguments on October 10, the jury returned the verdict: guilty of murder in the second degree. The sentence was pronounced by Judge Williams on October 12: to be "imprisoned in the State Prison at Auburn at hard labor for the term of your natural life."

There appears to have been much public sympathy for the doctor during the course of the trial. While in jail, the doctor was reported to have despaired at his plight. His wife was gone, his house was mortgaged and the bill of sale would have stripped the house of all comforts.

On October 14, Sheriff Brown left Herkimer to deliver Mary Druse—charged as an accessory to her mother Roxalana Druse's murder of her husband, William—and the doctor to their respective prisons. Dr. A. Walter Suiter also accompanied Richter. Mary reached her destination, the Onondaga County Penitentiary, first. The party then proceeded to Auburn, arriving at 4:05 p.m. Richter was assigned to "a light place in the hospital."

Dr. Moritz Richter died in prison on October 19, 1887, at the age of sixty-four. His body was brought back to Herkimer and buried at Oak Hill Cemetery. S. Clark Smith's funeral in the Methodist Episcopal Church of Herkimer was largely attended. Burial followed at Oak Hill Cemetery. Eliza Ward Richter continued as owner of the house purchased by the doctor in 1868.

QUARREL OVER A BUTTON

By Kelsey Denton

James Platts and Rufus Nichols Jr. were two neighbors involved in a homicide in the village of Herkimer in 1893. Platts was living in a tenement building on Prospect Street with his wife, Margaret, upstairs. He was around the age of fifty-six and was a carpenter. Nichols also resided in the same building downstairs with his wife, Anna, and son, Byron. He was around fifty-four years of age and worked for the railroad.

On June 11, 1893, at around 7:30 p.m., Nichols was shot in the leg by Platts in their house after a quarrel ensued between the pair. The source of the contention between the two? A button on their house front door.

Nichols did not like the door opening and slamming shut at late hours, waking him up at night, so he decided to put a button on the door to fasten it at night. Platts, on the other hand, did not like the button there. He did not want to have to go around to the back door when coming in at night and felt that he should not have to do so. When Nichols refused to take the button off, Platts grew angrier.

On the night of June 11, Platts came back to the house under the influence of alcohol, grabbed an axe or hammer and began banging on the button on the front door to remove it. When Nichols heard the banging, he immediately came to the door and confronted him about it. As they were both arguing, Platts pulled out his gun and pointed it at Nichols. Nichols pushed the gun down trying to get it away from him, but then was shot in his left leg, resulting in a wound in Nichols's upper thigh near his hip. The police and doctor were sent for. The two doctors who arrived were Dr. Kay and Dr. Casey, and the officer's name was Chief Manion. Nichols was found facedown bleeding profusely, and the doctors had to get the ball out of his leg. Unsuccessful, Nichols was sent to Faxton Hospital in Utica, where he was placed under the care of Dr. J.H. Glass. Nichols underwent a very serious operation at the hospital to remove his leg, which later resulted in gangrene, a severe bacterial infection resulting from the death of tissue in one area of the body. On the following Wednesday, June 14, 1893, this infection resulted in the death of Rufus Nichols around 1:15 a.m.

After the quarrel, Mr. Platts was brought into custody at the county jail after attempting to flee the scene. He stayed there until his trial was brought to the grand jury by Attorney General Devendorf in Herkimer in December. It was made known that not only did Mr. Platts commit this offense but also that he was arrested three times before, one time for stealing cigarettes and the other times for intoxication. Finally, on December 22, 1893, James Platts was found guilty of the murder of Rufus Nichols Jr. and charged with manslaughter in the first degree; he was sent to the Auburn prison for seventeen years. He served a term of ten years and seven months after his sentence was reduced for good behavior and returned to Herkimer in 1904.

VALE OF TEARS

By Gregg Lawrence

Carl "Fritz" Kloetzler, born in Germany, moved to this country and settled in New York City in about 1882. He had resided in Dolgeville for five years with his wife and four children in a house on the outskirts of town at 21 Spencer Street. He was a shoemaker by trade and was formerly employed in the felt department of the firm of Alfred Dolge & Son. Newspaper reports described his disposition as cross and sour and ugly in temperament; he had socialistic ideas with anarchistic tendencies. He was possessed of a goodly amount of intelligence, and it is said he was a regular correspondent to several anarchist papers. This is a depiction of a man who with coolness murdered his wife and four children on Friday, March 30, 1894.

The previous December, when the work decreased in the shoe factory, Kloetzler was thrown out of employment. After that, he did not work, although he might have secured some employment in a lumberyard or on public work had he asked for it. Over the preceding few months, he wrote several letters to Carl Fallier, a former shop mate who was in New York, saying he was tired of living and did not want to be a trouble to the people of Dolgeville. Each time, Fallier would respond positively, telling Kloetzler not to be discouraged, that business was on the gain and that he would be restored to his former position in the felt factory. In the latter part of February, Mrs. Kloetzler went to Henry Freygang, foreman of the shoe shop, and asked him to give her husband some work, as he was getting hostile and she feared that he would kill himself unless he was earning money. Mr. Freygang told her that there was no work for any of the men at that time, but as soon as he could consistently do so he would throw some work the way of her husband. This cheered her up a bit, and she told her husband that if he was patient they would have no cause to feel anxious about the future, as there was a prospect of his getting employment.

This promised opportunity to earn money did not come about, and a frenzied rage began building up inside of Kloetzler. He wrote to Fallier, stating that he intended to kill himself and his family. This letter Mr. Fallier took to Alfred Dolge, who immediately sent the following telegram to Dolgeville: "Kloetzler writes to Fallier that he will kill himself and family. Investigate at once and if necessary have him arrested to protect his family. His letter follows by mail. DOLGE."

This telegram was received by Edward Dedicke, and Chief of Police James Cramer was at once notified of its contents. Kloetzler had many times made similar threats before to other persons, and earlier in the week, Alfred Dolge's personal attorney, Edward A. Brown, warned Cramer to keep a watch on the man, fearing that something would happen in the household. Mr. Brown's warning was later followed up with a request to arrest Kloetzler.

Dedicke also contacted attorney George W. Ward and George Kneaskern, one of the employees of the Dolge firm. The telegram was received at noon, and at about one o'clock, Chief Cramer visited the Kloetzler house on the pretense of renting it, as he had heard that Kloetzler intended to move away. The latter had told his neighbors that he intended to start for Boston the next day. For weeks, Kloetzler had engaged in selling and giving away his furniture, and all that remained was a few chairs, a kitchen stove and a little bedding. Kloetzler received Cramer good-naturedly and, when informed of his errand, allowed Cramer about the house. Cramer remained about an hour visiting the family and saw nothing to arouse suspicion that anything was wrong.

Cramer came down the street and met Dedicke and said it was "all bosh," that Kloetzler would leave in the morning and all was all right. Dedicke was not yet satisfied and got Mr. Ward to go to the house. Ward went there in the afternoon and was admitted by Kloetzler. Ward wanted to know if there was anything that he could do for him and asked if Kloetzler had enough money to pay his expenses. Kloetzler said he had about thirty-two dollars. Ward said he would see Poormaster Sidney Ransom and give him ten dollars more so his family would not be destitute. Then Ward left around four o'clock, saw Dedicke and said he did not think there was anything to it.

After Ward left, Kloetzler went out for a stroll, and those he encountered said he did not appear as if he was making up his mind to end his life. In answer to all questions on when he was leaving Dolgeville, Kloetzler answered that he was going Saturday morning at nine o'clock. He added in a joking voice to one friend, "Tonight, me and my family will sleep for the last time in Dolgeville, and we will sleep like Italians—all in one bed."

At about seven o'clock, Mr. Ward went back to see Kloetzler along with Mr. Ransom and remained until 8:30 p.m. Mrs. Kloetzler was washing the children before a fire in the living room. "We want them to be clean for the morning," she said. Clean clothes were also placed and packed in a satchel ready to lay them out. They also noticed that the window facing the next house was covered with a bedsheet, which seemed strange to them. During the time Ward and Ransom were at the home, Kloetzler drank a cup of black coffee and gave his children some of it. Ransom insisted on Kloetzler showing the money with which he intended to go to Long Island, his aforementioned destination. Kloetzler refused, saying that it was not stolen and that it was his. At times, when driven very close, Kloetzler was mad and inclined to be ugly. Ransom told Kloetzler they would gladly help him move if they wanted help, but Kloetzler's eyes blazed with a dangerous, maddened light. Although no threats had been made toward them, they feared Kloetzler and his anarchistic reputation, and they left and went down the street, intending to get Officer Cramer and send him to the house to either arrest Kloetzler or remain with him all night.

During the time Ward and Ransom were at the Kloetzler house, the editors of the *New York Volkszeitung*, the daily German socialist newspaper of that city, received a letter from Fritz Kloetzler, stating that he was about to commit a terrible and desperate deed. He said in the letter that he had been driven frantic by poverty and misfortune. "I have a wife and four children," he wrote. "I will kill them and then will kill myself! Oh, this life is hellish! I must do it: When you get this letter I and mine will be no more."

The editors of the *Volkszeitung* immediately wired to Dolgeville, and at about eight o'clock, the telephone operator received the following over the long-distance line: "Kloetzler sent a letter to a New York paper in which he stated he intended killing his own family and then committing suicide."

The desperate man's letter to the *Volkszeitung* opens with these words: "When you receive these lines six human hearts will have ceased beating. Five years ago, I came from New York City to this most miserable town of Dolgeville. Whoever cannot be a humbug, a swindler and spy will never be able to make a decent living. Whenever there is anybody who does not say aye, aye to whatever the omnipotent master may say in public speeches will be placed upon the black list and discharged at the first opportunity."

Kloetzler said in his letter that he never did wrong or injured anybody, but he was discharged for what he knew not. His wife was sick, it was Christmas when he got sick and he alleged he made every effort to find work elsewhere in vain. "Now as my wife is too sick to do any housework and as I am suffering from dyspepsia it is impossible for me to do any hard work either, we have decided to leave this vale of tears together. It was terrible for us to agree that we also should take with us our four hopeful children. But my wife is of the same opinion with me that our offspring should not fall victim to these monsters. We did not want them to be like us."

Ward and Ransom found Cramer, who then went after Constable Wallace Fish. This took about twenty minutes. In the meantime, Joseph

Tyo, a neighbor, went to the house for the purpose of bidding Kloetzler goodbye. During the time he was there, two of the children appeared dumpish and sleepy and were taken upstairs to bed by Kloetzler. It was about nine o'clock when Cramer, Fish, Ward, Ransom, Kneaskern, E.S. Schermerhorn and Dedicke returned to the house. The doors were all locked, and lights were burning downstairs and upstairs. Repeated knocking brought no response. Going to a side door, Kneaskern unlocked the door with a key, and a trembling Ward, Cramer and Fish entered the house. The lower rooms were vacated, and a hot fire was burning in the stove. They called loudly for Kloetzler, but no response came. Finally, Ward, with lamp in hand, followed by the two officers, started up the stairs. There they beheld one of the most ghastly, sickening sights that man has ever witnessed.

On a cheap hair-filled mattress with their heads near the wall lay the six in a bloody row. On the north end of the room was the wife, Ida, with a deep gash in her throat—her hair laid back under her head and her face turned to the south to give her husband a clear chance at her jugular vein. Her right arm had traces of the blood of her daughter that had burst on her as the girl was being killed by her father. Next was the eldest daughter, Freida, age twelve, with her throat cut, embracing her mother, her face besmeared with the thin stream of her mother's blood. Next came Elsie, age three, killed by poison; then Paul, age eight, killed by poison, his arm lovingly around the slim neck of Elsie; and lastly Bruno, the youngest son, age six, his throat cut, nearly severing his head from the body. All were in their nightclothes and covered up with blankets, with blood-saturated clothing for a pillow; their faces were dotted with the blood of their father and other members of the family. On top of the blanket between Freida and Elsie lay the murderer. His coat was off, his hands and arms covered with the blood of his wife and children. He had a gash across his throat, and his wrist was cut, which was determined to be the fatal wound; he had finished by plunging the knife into his heart. The knife was drawn out and thrown near the head of his wife as Kloetzler drew his hands together and folded them over his breast to meet his fate. The knife used was a shoemaker's knife used in trimming, about a foot long and with a five-inch blade. It was as sharp as a razor.

At the foot of the mattress on the floor was a pot of coffee laced with arsenic, an empty pint bottle and a dipper half full of water. Upon searching the house, a package of white powder that had recently been opened was found, and in the stove hearth there was a paper evidently taken from it, on which was a label marked "Arsenic" and bore the stamp of J.B. Stone, 11 West Fulton Streer, Gloversville. In the front room downstairs were three saucers on an old box containing a substance resembling paste mixed up. In the saucers were spoons, and one of them was entirely empty. The supposition is that this was the poison that had been given to the family.

During the search of the Kloetzler house, Edward Dedicke found two letters, one addressed to Alfred Dolge and the other to Adolph Freygang. Both were written in German, the same threatening message as the *Volkszeitung* letter, with Kloetzler stating he would destroy himself rather than work for a dollar a day. The letter also said that he was going to kill himself and his family to leave a black mark for Dolgeville and Alfred Dolge.

In the week prior to the murders, Kloetzler had realized $62.25 from the sale of his furniture. He had sent the $32 he alleged to possess to Carl Fallier and also sent him an express package. He sent the balance of the money to a woman in Long Island.

Coroner E.H. Douglass of Little Falls arrived in Dolgeville on March 31, examined the bodies in the house and empaneled the following jury: Ed S. Schermerhorn, foreman, along with W.F. Stoddard, W.H. Bacon, Wheeler Knapp, L. Hutton, R.J. Guile, M. Drake, M.A. Barrett, J.C. Spofford, Charles Dedicke, Fred Johnson and Edward Munk. The jury viewed the remains, and the inquest commenced at Vedder Hall.

The Kloetzler family were buried at the village cemetery on Sunday, April 1. The funeral services were held at three o'clock in the house where the murders were committed, with undertaker R.J. McDougal in charge. The crowd of about four hundred that assembled expressed much sympathy for the fate that befell the four children, but no words of pity were spoken for the husband and wife. There was a short prayer by Reverend Mr. Watson, a hymn by the Methodist Episcopal church choir and the benediction. Then the five coffins—the toddler being buried with her mother—were placed in two wagons and conveyed to the Dolgeville cemetery and buried together in one large grave. To this day, there are no official records of the location where the bodies are buried at the cemetery. It has been rumored that they were buried in unconsecrated grounds, that the caretaker refused to tend to the grave and that the area became overgrown through the years.

The coroner's inquest in the matter of the death of the Kloetzler family was concluded on April 2. Drs. Strobel and Getman testified regarding the findings of their examination, and the jury rendered a verdict that the wife

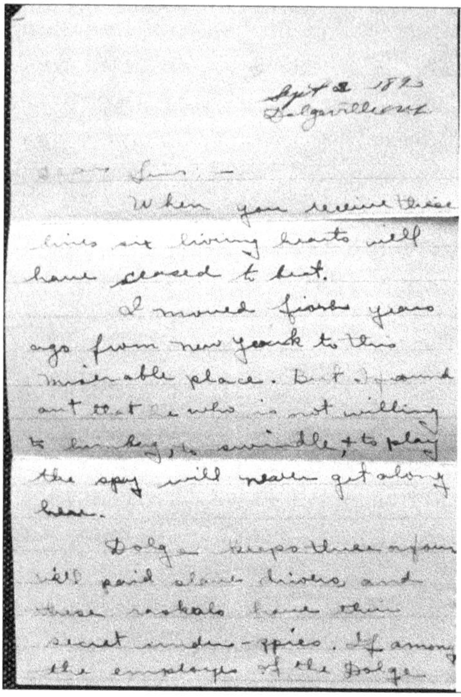

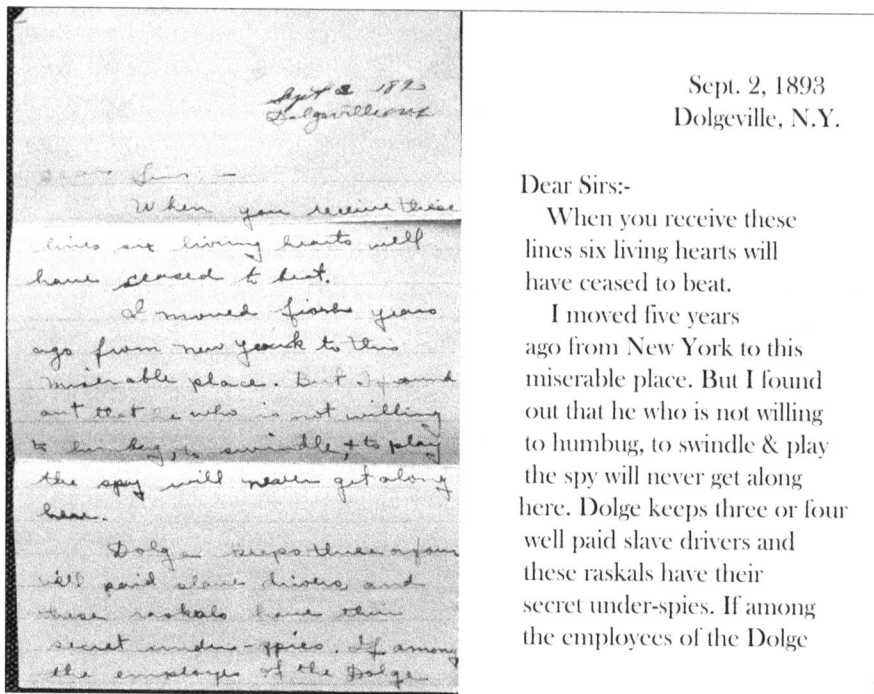

Sept. 2, 1893
Dolgeville, N.Y.

Dear Sirs:-
When you receive these lines six living hearts will have ceased to beat.
I moved five years ago from New York to this miserable place. But I found out that he who is not willing to humbug, to swindle & play the spy will never get along here. Dolge keeps three or four well paid slave drivers and these raskals have their secret under-spies. If among the employees of the Dolge

The first page of the original letter that Kloetzler wrote telling of his intentions.

and children had come to their deaths at the hands of Fritz Kloetzler and that Kloetzler came to his death by a knife wound inflicted by his own hand. The jury also found that Mrs. Kloetzler was a party to and had knowledge of the entire plot. After careful examination, the jury also found the village authorities were not negligent in their duties.

As if this tragic tale could not be any more gruesome, a shocking discovery was made a few months later. On May 18, it is believed by police authorities that Fritz Kloetzler also murdered an infant child of his. When the outhouse was cleaned at the Kloetzler house, the decomposed body of an infant was found. It is believed that Kloetzler's wife gave birth to a child and that it was thrown where it was found.

A letter has recently been discovered, 125 years later, by a person going through the personal belongings of a family in Portland, Oregon, who used to have old family ties to Dolgeville. The letter is similar in nature to the *Volkszeitung* letter, written in the hand of Fritz Kloetzler and dated September 2, 1893, almost six months before the murders:

Dear Sir,

When you receive these lines six living hearts will have ceased to beat.

I moved five years ago from New York to this miserable place. But I found out that he who is not willing to humbug, to swindle, & to play the spy will never get along here.

Dolge keeps three or four well paid slave drivers, and these raskals have their secret under-spies. If among the employees of the Dolge factory, anyone is found who does not approve of everything done by the all-powerful ruler of Dolgeville, and all the pretty sounding speeches that he promises from time to time, such employees are forthwith placed on the black list and are discharged at the first opportunity, Alltho' there was no charge against me and alltho Dolge as everyone else in the village knows that I had to support a sickly wife and four little children, I was last Christmas discharged by order of the black list. The obstensible grounds was that business was slack. I tried my best to get work in other places but in vain.

In view of this and further circumstances that my wife is too ill to attend to the household and that my own stomach in disposition does not allow me to do hard work, she and I have agreed to depart this vale of tears. Our greatest apprehension is about our four little, good, hopeful children never the less neither my wife nor I wished they should fall into the hands of some capitalist to be fleeced as wage slaves. If in any way I had behaved inappropriately, I would long ago have gone to Dolge and begged him to give me work alltho' the wages are only one dollar a day. But I was discharged upon no good grounds and I prefer to die a thousand times rather than to serve a good word for this dangerous and despicable fleecer of working men.

Externally Dolge is a friend to the working man but in fact their worst enemy.

Of the $500 he is said to have "given" the poor last January, no one has got a cent. It all went right back into his own pockets. May our death be a curse on this Dolge and this whole kit. May everything this fellow under takes wither in his hand, may he too feel someday hunger gnawing in his stomach as so many others now do who have been thrown into misery by his accursed system.

This fellow aims in getting into Congress. Workingmen, I pray you do not give your vote to this man. You have no idea what a false man this Dolge is; he thinks his will is supreme and is the counterpart of the present Boy-Emperor of Germany. He is ready to crush whoever does not bow to his will.

Enclosed dear sir, .50 cents with request that you send copies of your esteemed paper to the following addresses (names to follow) if you would have the kindness to print this letter.

With my last writing, Fritz Kloetzler

JEALOUS LOVER: THE ELLA AUSMAN MURDER

By Angela Harris

I am 29 years of age; I reside in Frankfort; Orchard Street, No 5; I have been in Little Falls five years; I have lived here, No 46 John street* [the Wolcott home] *for four years. Morris Jackson came to Mrs.* [Harvey] *Hartman's house, No 48 about half-past six. He came there and called for me. He wanted to call upon me; I went to the door; I told him I didn't want to see him. He asked me to state some evening when he could call upon me. I told him I didn't wish him to call on me any more. He said, "Ella, you don't know what you are doing." I told him if I ever wanted him to call again I would write him. At that he said good bye and went out of the house. I take my meals as Mrs. Hartman's house at No. 48 John street; I have my room at No. 46. I went to the table* [at Mrs. Hartman's] *for my supper and Morris Jackson came in and fired a revolver. I can't tell whether he fired at me or at Mr. McIntosh, who was sitting at the table. I got up and ran over here* [no. 46 John Street]…*before I got up he fired again. I was hit but can't tell whether it was the first or second time he fired. I came right over here; I told my people I was shot and my people sent for the doctor and an officer. Mrs. Nettie Hartman, Fred McIntosh, Mrs. Frank Cronkhite, Mrs. Eaton, Mr.* [Charles] *Persons, were in the room when the shooting occurred.*

Morris Jackson shot Ella Ausman and Fred McIntosh at 6:30 p.m. on January 28, 1897. The preceding, dispassionate statement by Ella Ausman was recorded in the presence of Coroner Geo. S. Eveleth and Recorder Alonzo H. Green on January 28. She made her statement before doctors "put her under" to prepare for surgery. Drs. Douglass and Ingham removed the bullet, and at 7:30 p.m., the operation was declared a "decided success." Unfortunately, that determination did not prove true.

ELLA M. AUSMAN.

MORRIS JACKSON.

Ella Ausman was a button-hole machine operator at the Eagle Mill owned by the Honorable Titus Sheard in Little Falls, where she had worked for five years. As her statement indicated, she was from Frankfort and still considered that her permanent home, although she was born in Herkimer and attended school there. Morris Jackson was apparently unemployed at the time he shot Miss Ausman. He arrived in Little Falls from Middleville at least five years before the shooting.

Jackson had worked on the New York Central Railroad, and after quitting that job, he worked as a bartender in Little Falls. With another man, he leased and operated a bar in a space at the back of the New York Central Station, but he left that business about a month before the shooting.

It is not clear how long Miss Ausman and Mr. Jackson had been seeing each other, but it may have been as long as five years. One report noted that not long before the final episode in their relationship, she had returned a gold ring to him, telling him that she did not wish to spend time with him anymore. He is said to have thrown the ring to the ground and stomped on it. There are also reports that he had spoken to McIntosh on several occasions, demanding that he not bestow attentions on Ella Ausman.

Mr. Fred McIntosh roomed at Mrs. Thorpe's house on John Street, in the same block as Mrs. Nettie Hartman's boardinghouse, where both he and Miss Ausman took their meals. This may have been the extent of their interaction, but Morris Jackson became quite jealous of Ella Ausman when she sought to terminate their relationship. As she herself recounted, one evening in January, Jackson stopped at the Hartman house to speak to Ausman and perhaps rekindle her affection. When she rejected him again, he left and returned about fifteen minutes later, carrying a .38-caliber revolver with five chambers.

FRED M'INTOSH

Jackson first shot McIntosh, then Ella Ausman and then himself. Four shots were fired. The first hit McIntosh in the wrist. Jackson grabbed Ausman around the neck from behind and pointed the gun against her chest and fired. The bullet bounced off her steel corset stays and splintered, then entered her body near her heart. He turned the gun on himself and shot, but the bullet was found later lodged in his clothing after he was in jail. A bullet, found on the floor under the table, was probably fired after the bullet that hit McIntosh.

Ausman ran next door to the Wolcott house, where she rented a room. Her landlady called for a doctor and an officer. The remaining people in the Hartmann dining room tried to hide during the shooting, but after Ausman ran out, Mr. Pearsons jumped Jackson and wrestled him to the floor with the aid of the bleeding McIntosh. The other diners helped restrain him until the officer arrived.

Dr. E.H. Douglass was summoned to the site of the shooting to find that Officer Long had arrived. Ausman was treated at her rooming house by Drs. Ingraham and Douglass, who expected her to make a full recovery. Jackson was taken to the county jail in Herkimer, where he was originally charged with two counts of attempted murder since both Ausman and McIntosh were expected to recover. At the time, the assumption was that he would be convicted and be sentenced to ten years in prison.

Ella Ausman did not improve. At 3:00 a.m. on the morning of the thirtieth, her condition began to deteriorate. The doctors were called, as were Chief O'Rourke, District Attorney Richardson and Recorder Greene. Richardson arrived on the 9:00 a.m. train and presided at her final statement. By then, she was having trouble seeing and hearing, but although that statement was not released, it was reported to be much the same as the original. Ausman's mother and family members and Reverend Dr. Richardson of the Presbyterian church were called to her bedside.

Ella Ausman died at 4:30 p.m. on Saturday, January 30, forty-six hours after the shooting. An autopsy was performed on January 31, with an inquest held on February 1. Her funeral was held on February 2 at her parents' home in Frankfort, with Reverend Robert Fletcher, rector of St. Albans, speaking.

On February 7, Fred D. McIntosh was discharged from the hospital, where he had recovered completely from his injuries. Jackson was held at the Herkimer jail. He was indicted for first-degree murder on April 7, 1897, and held for trial. He entered a plea of not guilty. During his early stay at the Herkimer jail, other inmates reported him to be despairing, moaning and berating himself throughout the day and night. He was visited regularly by his mother but, save for one or two exceptions, refused to talk to news reporters.

In September 1897, the court determined that it would be impossible to proceed with the trial before the regular term in December because the Supreme Court judges were unavailable. The county prosecutor prepared for trial in March 1898. Jackson was represented by the Honorable Eugene E. Seldon and George E. Thomas, while Deputy Attorney General Arleigh D. Richardson was to be assisted by A.M. Mills of Little Falls as prosecutors. In an attempt to empanel a jury, five hundred men from the towns of Herkimer County were called up, at some expense to the county.

On March 14, 1898, with a third panel of two hundred jurors in attendance to be interviewed, Charles D. Thomas, for the defense, addressed the court, reviewing the crime and its effects on the family of the defendant; he asked that the court accept a plea of guilty of murder in the second degree. Mr. Mills spoke for the prosecution, recommending that the court accept that change in plea. Judge McLennan accepted the plea and Jackson assented. The two days' delay before sentencing was waived, and Morris Jackson was sentenced to imprisonment at Auburn State Prison for the "term of his natural life."

Morris Jackson was taken to Auburn by Sheriff Baker on March 16, 1898. The following December, the county clerk reported that the trial that didn't happen had cost the county $6,000. And Ella Ausman had been dead for more than a year.

**Birth records indicate that Ella was born in April 1862, making her age thirty-five at the time of her death. At least one other report lists her age as thirty-one.*

NELLIE HAD A DATE WITH DEATH

By Peg Masters, Town of Webb Historian

Nellie Widrick had "a roving disposition," reported a Utica newspaper several days after she was brutally bludgeoned to death with an axe on September 21, 1899. The murder took place at a lumber camp boardinghouse near Old Forge in northern Herkimer County. Her alleged killer, Horace Norton, fled the scene southward along the railroad tracks by the Moose River, according to a camp boarder. All through the night, Nellie's body lay on the ground below the porch steps. A coroner from Frankfort finally arrived to conduct an inquest. Nellie's right ear was severed, and the left side of her face had been crushed by a bloody axe found at the scene.

Horace P. Norton was captured ten days later, hiding in a barn near Turin, New York. While he awaited his trial in the Herkimer County Jail, reporters scrambled to uncover more details about the couple. Horace was about forty-five years old according to authorities, the son of a well-respected Turin hop grower. By the age of eighteen, he was married to Dora Burdick, who gave birth to their son, Henry, in 1878. Dora died two years later shortly after the birth of their daughter, Alice. Horace's second wife, Lidia C. Loveland, had been an inmate at Ogdensburg Insane Asylum for several years. Early in September 1899, Norton coerced Nellie into leaving her job husking corn at a canning factory in Camden, pretending to be his wife and working as a cook at Henry Bridgman's lumber camp.

A funeral was held for Helen "Nellie" Widrick at her mother Sarah's home in Camden. Her remains were interred at Pineville Cemetery, Oswego County, where her father, Solomon C. Widrick, and her sister, Hattie, were buried. Disparaging details emerged that Nellie was Norton's "paramour." She had never divorced her last husband and had also been involved with several other men from the Camden area. Her hometown newspaper issued the gentlest report: "What her life has been is now in the past and a mantle of charity should be thrown over it. With all her faults, Miss Widrick was a kind-hearted woman in time of sickness or trouble, and the neighbors speak of her many helpful acts."

The widely anticipated trial convened in February 1900, with Justice Maurice L. Wright presiding. He instructed the prosecutor, District Attorney Adam J. Smith, to summon an extra-large panel of 150 potential jurors. It took an entire week to seat 12 men. Horace Norton faced the death penalty if he were convicted of the first-degree murder charge. Two of Herkimer's

The scene of the crime.

finest barristers, the Honorable Abram B. Steele and Charles D. Thomas, were assigned by Judge Wright to defend Horace Norton.

Prosecutor Smith's case rested on convincing jurors that the motive for the murder was jealousy. During an argument on the day of the murder, Horace had accused Nellie of being flirtatious with another boarder. A witness from Camden testified that in early September, he overheard Norton threaten to kill Nellie if she did not go with him. Mr. and Mrs. Bridgman both took the stand and said that they had witnessed the couple's argument. Before they went to bed that night, Mrs. Bridgman told the defendant, "Mr. Norton, you have no reason to be jealous of Nellie since she has been here." Jurors heard testimonies from the coroner who conducted the inquest, the deputy sheriff who arrested Horace in Turin and a forensic expert who found hair, blood and brain samples on the axe.

Horace Norton and Nellie Widrick.

Nellie's mother, Sarah, was the final witness for the prosecution. On cross-examination, Mr. Steele pelted her with questions about her daughter's lifestyle and previous relationships with men. During the previous year, Nellie had gone to Glenfield to work as Norton's housekeeper, and Sarah thought they were married. Judge Wright finally called a halt to Mr. Steele's line of questioning. The possibility that the victim may have been partially responsible for her own death, however, had become imbedded in the minds of the jurors.

Defense attorney Charles D. Thomas's opening statement brought tears to his client's eyes. "We will show you the character of the defendant from his school days up to the present time—a character that any of you jurymen might envy." Horace's father, John; son, Henry; daughter, Alice; and several other relatives were in attendance throughout the trial. A sister of Horace's second wife stated that she considered him a brother and that he had always been kind to Lidia. A half dozen or so more witnesses testified to Norton's good character. When called to the stand, Henry Norton admitted that he saw his father on the road the night after Nellie was murdered, but their conversation was not allowed to go into evidence.

On the final day of the trial, Horace's sister-in-law pinned a bouquet of flowers on his lapel and gave him a kiss. The Honorable Abram. B. Steele gave an enervated closing statement: "There is no evidence of deliberation or premeditation. If he killed her, he did it in a frenzy." The defendant wept, as did his whole family, with one notable exception: his son, Henry Norton. It took the jury six hours of deliberation to find Horace Norton guilty of second-degree murder.

Horace's two children died while he was serving out a life sentence at the Auburn prison, where he worked as a cook and a carpenter. In May 1916, he was transferred to Great Meadows Prison in Comstock, Washington County, and subsequently was paroled. For several years, he worked nearby in Whitehall as a carpenter. Horace P. Norton died in Voorheesville, New York, on April 14, 1925. The Bridgman boardinghouse was dismantled and reconstructed where it stands today near the railroad station on the outskirts of Old Forge. At the insistence of the longtime homeowner, the front entrance was boarded up. She never wanted to cross the threshold where Nellie Widrick met her date with death on that fateful September night more than a century ago.

THE CASE OF INFANTICIDE

By Susan Perkins

This sad case came to light when a letter was sent to District Attorney George Ward on August 2, 1902, signed by the "Citizens of Salisbury." The letter stated the following: "There is a case here in Salisbury Corners that should be looked into at once in the home of David Edwards, who has had this woman living with his family twelve or fifteen years and she within the past week has given birth to a child. But it has not been seen and is believed murdered. This has been done again and again and research should be done at once. Mrs. E. could give you all the information necessary if she will tell what she knows. Kindly give this your prompt attention."

It was rumored that Vida A. Harper Phelps, the widow of John Phelps (who died in 1888), lived in the household of David and Elizabeth Edwards and their five daughters. In the household also lived a ten-year-old boy named Fayette, who was the son of Edwards but went by the last name of Phelps. Elizabeth Edwards, David's wife, knew of the illicit affair. It was alleged that when Elizabeth protested about the affair, her husband told her that she might leave if she chose but that the other woman would stay. Three times Vida gave birth to infants who disappeared. There wasn't a doctor or midwife present at the births.

The Edwards family and Vida lived at Salisbury Corners at the time of the last birth. Mrs. Edwards and Vida worked on the Thompson farm together. When Vida's condition was noticed by Mrs. Edwards, she questioned her husband and Vida, but they were reticent. On Friday night, July 25, 1902, Vida stayed in her room until Monday, July 28, when she came downstairs and went right back up until Wednesday. On Thursday, Mrs. Edwards noticed a lot of bloodstained clothing in the woodshed that was washed later on by Vida and removed. An investigation ensued, and Mr. Edwards was arrested by the district attorney. Edwards denied any "improper relations between himself and Mrs. Phelps." Mr. Edwards was about forty-five years of age, rough in manners and unattractive, having only one eye. He had been married for more than twenty years.

The authorities went to the farm of James Thompson, where Vida was working, to question her. She broke down and told her shocking story in sickening detail. Vida had been warned by Edwards that the baby must not be allowed to live. The baby was born on the night of Saturday, July 26. Vida had made no attempt to check hemorrhage from the infant at the umbilical cord. She covered it under the bedsheets until its cries ceased and it no longer breathed. She placed the remains in a satchel that she left under the bed. On Monday, she informed Edwards of the deed. She concealed the body until that Thursday, when she buried the infant behind the woodshed. But fearing discovery she disinterred it and took it into the shed. She moved a pile of wood and pulled up the floorboards, burying the baby there and then replacing the floorboards and wood. The investigators found the baby well preserved in the dry earth. The remains were of a healthy seven-and-a-half-pound baby boy. Vida then admitted to killing a child born two years earlier on the Miller place in Salisbury, burying it in front of the cow stalls. The *Evening Times* wrote, "Six years ago she interred another below a beam in a barn on the Avery farm in Fairfield, where they then lived. She alleges that she was under the influence of Edwards. The latter, while making no confession, is stated to assert as an offset that he was under the woman's influence. She confirms that he is the father of the boy Fayette and asserted that it was by his advice and urging in each instance that she took the lives of the children. She is a woman of about thirty years, a brunette and of coarse appearance." They were issued warrants on a charge of murder in the first degree by the coroner. They were taken to the Herkimer jail.

The trial started on January 8, 1903. Mr. Edwards was charged with infanticide. The first witness was Dr. A.O. Douglass of Little Falls, followed by Drs. Eveleth and E.H. Douglas, who testified to finding the infant's body in the woodshed and to the condition of the body as disclosed by the autopsy.

Vida testified on January 9 in great detail of the horrible crime. On January 10, David Edwards was found guilty. He was indicted for manslaughter in the second degree in causing the death of a newborn child in Salisbury during the summer. He was sentenced on January 12. He was admitted to the Auburn prison for six years and two months on January 22, 1903.

On January 16, Vida was found guilty of manslaughter. She was sentenced to the Auburn prison for a minimum of one year and a maximum of three years and was admitted on January 22, 1903.

After David served his sentence, he came back to live with his wife and two of his five daughters in the town of Manheim. He died on May 23, 1930, and is buried at the Salisbury Rural Cemetery.

Vida was released from prison on May 22, 1905. In 1905, Vida and son Fayette were living in the household of Edward Everson in the town of Salisbury. In 1915, Vida and Fayette were living in Dolgeville at 17 Elm Street. She died of a heart attack on May 5, 1919, on the train between Dolgeville and Salisbury Center while talking to the conductor. She is buried at the Salisbury Rural Cemetery.

AN UNUSUAL TRAGEDY

By Wendy Ladd Weeks

The *Saturday Globe*'s caption for this murder story read, "An Unusual Tragedy." One cannot read the account without feeling the utmost regret and deep sympathy for everyone involved.

Two boys were living on the Percy B. Budlong farm located east of Utica on Route 5 in the town of Schuyler. Herbert W. Moon, a youth of only thirteen years, had shot and killed Lucian Drew, a young man of eighteen. The only eyewitness was the hired maidservant, Mary Hayes.

Lucian had been hired in May 1903 by the Budlong family to help with the farm chores. According to newspaper accounts, he had left his family and hometown of Ithaca, Michigan, and had traveled east with a theatrical troupe prior to his arrival in Schuyler. Did Lucian run away from home because he was a stubborn independent child, or was he out seeking a job to help out the family at home?

Young Herbert had a previous scrape with the law. He had committed petit larceny by stealing money from his stepmother, causing him to be committed to the Rochester Industrial School in August 1902 at the age of twelve. According to the testimony made by his father, Delavan W. Moon, Herbert was released after four months from the school for good behavior. By the summer of 1903, his stepmother had made arrangements with Percy and Lora Budlong to board Herbert at their home. It was thought that living outside the city would provide "better influences"[14] during the summer.

Was Herbert a troublesome child or was he acting out because his father, a traveling salesman, and his new (young) stepmother did not provide a stable home life?

The lone witness to the murder was Miss Mary Hayes, the hired servant. Mr. and Mrs. Budlong, both in their mid-twenties, had one toddler at the time, little Bessie. Having a few young men around the farm and a young lady as a domestic certainly seemed to be reasonable assurance that things would be fine at the house while the Budlongs rode into Utica on Tuesday morning, August 20, 1903.

Mary Hayes's accounts during her testimony and those of other witnesses illustrate how in just a few months the quarrelsome, bickering boys developed ill feelings toward each other—whether from envy, besting or resentful justifications. In most occasions, this was normal "boys will be boys" behavior. Unfortunately, in this case, the quarrels escalated into violence.

In the late morning, according to Mary Hayes's story, she went down to the lot to get a pail of potatoes. When she came back, each of the boys was accusing the other of rummaging about the house and eating honey from the pantry. Herbert said Drew had gone through Mr. Budlong's desk and his dresser. The girl paid no attention to their complaints. Then Drew demanded something to eat, and she set out some rolls and honey for the two in the kitchen. "Why did you tell Mary I was snooping, Lucian," demanded Herbert, "when you did it yourself, and ate the honey too?"

HERBERT MOON.

LUCIAN DREW.

"If you say I ate it, Lucian replied, "you lie." "I don't lie" was the boy's response. "You're the liar."[15]

Mary furthered the account of the incident by testifying that Lucian grabbed Herbert by the neck, choking him until Herbert was able to kick himself loose, running into the parlor. There Lucian again attacked Herbert with a chair and continued to choke him violently. At this point, Mary went to seek help but returned without doing so. Meanwhile, Lucian ran back into the kitchen and held the door closed to keep Herbert from leaving the parlor. Once Lucian let go of the doorknob, both boys ran outside, with Lucian exiting the kitchen and Herbert through the front parlor. Although Mary had said she hid the gun in fear of the boys, Herbert managed to find it. Now, with all three of them outside the house, Mary heard Herbert, standing behind the house near the pump, say, "I'll blow your d----d brains out."[16] Lucian, about sixty feet away nearing the gate adjacent to the barn, turned "his head half around and shouted, 'Fire away. I ain't afraid.'"[17] The .22-caliber, rim-fire cartridge shot from the Steven rifle and blew into the base of Lucian's brain. He was dead within thirty minutes.

Lucian's father, Joseph Drew, arrived by train Friday, August 23, to collect his son's body and take it back for burial at the Baptist Church

MISS MARY HAYES.

INTERIOR OF THE BUDLONG KITCHEN.
[Where the fight between the boys began which ended in a tragedy.]

Cemetery in Alma, Michigan. Herbert Moon was immediately locked up in the Herkimer County Jail pending the grand jury decision for the charge of murder in the second degree. Through his attorney, Mr. Charles Thomas, Herbert waived examination. On December 23, Herbert's attorney asked the court to accept a plea of manslaughter in the second degree. Mr. Thomas also called attention "to Section 699 of the Penal Code, which provides that when a child under 14 is charged with a crime, which if committed as an adult would be a felon,"[18] the court may use discretion and try the child for a misdemeanor with appropriate sentence imposed. Judge Scripture denied this action, and the plea of manslaughter was accepted. The judge sentenced Herbert to return to the Rochester Industrial School, also known as the Western New York House of Refuge of Juvenile Delinquents. This seems to have been a fairly lenient sentence, as an adult felon would most assuredly have been sent to prison.

SCENE OF AN UNUSUAL TRAGEDY NEAR UTICA.

Due to the laws set out in the Health Insurance Portability and Accountability Act, nothing more is on record of Herbert Moon that can be researched. The annual report of the school noted that sometimes older boys were transferred to Elmira Reformatory if they proved incorrigible. Being this was Herbert's second offense, this may have been his fate. However, due to his youth, he may have remained there until perhaps being "paroled" to his parents, guardians or employer.

A *Saturday Globe* journalist's words echo a cautionary refrain for some even today more than a century later: "[T]hese are the consequences of an unusual tragedy which shocked central New York this week. It has its lesson. Perhaps that is the feature of the case which ought most to be considered and the weight of which should be borne in upon parents in an unforgettable manner. It is the folly of permitting children not yet out of school to handle firearms."[19]

The Budlong house still sits on Herkimer Road next to the Schuyler town office building. Lucian Drew's gravestone can be seen on the Find A Grave website. Herbert Moon, whose fate is unknown, may forever be lost except in the history of this story.

CHESTER GILLETTE

By Jack Sherman

In April 1905, Chester Gillette arrived in Cortland, New York, and began employment as manager of the stockroom of the Gillette Skirt Factory, owned by his uncle. Chester was twenty-one years old, handsome and well traveled and exuded an easy charm that placed him comfortably in the Cortland social scene. Chester quickly developed parallel lives: his public life, attending parties and dances with the higher echelon of Cortland society, and his secretive life, conducting a passionate affair with Grace Brown, a nineteen-year-old skirt inspector at his uncle's factory.

In the early spring of 1906, Grace revealed to Chester that she was pregnant with their child; she quit her job and moved back to her family's home in South Otselic. From there she wrote several beseeching letters to Chester, begging him to take her away and somehow resolve their situation. Chester responded coldly to these emotional letters and merely advised Grace to be patient, without any explicit plan to resolve their dilemma. However, when Grace threatened to come back to Cortland and reveal their situation publicly, Chester finally promised to meet her and travel together to the Adirondacks. The specific purpose of this trip was not discussed in their correspondence, although it seems likely that Grace expected that Chester would save her honor by marrying her.

On July 9, 1906, Chester and Grace met in DeRuyter, New York. They boarded a train to Utica, sitting separately. On the train, Chester met two young women he knew well from the Cortland social set who were headed for a vacation on Seventh Lake in the Adirondacks. Chester told them he was meeting a friend in the same area and would attempt to visit them by the end of the week.

Chester and Grace departed the train in Utica and spent the evening of July 9 at the Hotel Martin. Chester registered them as husband and wife under false names. They left early the next morning, July 10, without paying their bill and took a train north to the Adirondacks. They eventually arrived at Tupper Lake and stayed at the Alta Cliff Hotel that evening. Again, Chester registered them under false names as husband and wife.

The next morning, July 11, Chester and Grace took an early train headed south. Grace's trunk was checked through to Old Forge, near Fourth Lake. However, they decided to leave the train at the Big Moose Lake station, a few miles north of Old Forge, and were transported by wagon to the

Left: Chester Gillette. This photograph was taken after his arrest by Herkimer photographer Albert P. Zintsmaster.

Right: Grace Brown.

Glenmore Hotel at the western end of Big Moose Lake. When Chester signed the register at the Glenmore, for the first time he registered Grace with her actual name and address but signed himself in as "Carl Grahm, Albany, N.Y."

Chester rented a rowboat, and at about 11:00 a.m., they began to travel easterly on the lake, with Chester's suitcase between them—including a strapped-on tennis racket. They rowed about the lake all day, apparently making stops to pick waterlilies and eat lunch. They were last seen headed toward an eastern area of South Bay where no cottages existed, a point of land obscured from observation.

After Chester and Grace failed to return the rowboat that evening to the Glenmore, a search party was dispatched the next morning to find them. The overturned boat and Grace's body were discovered, but a continued search for "Carl Grahm" proved fruitless. Grace's body was transported south to Frankfort for an autopsy conducted by several physicians, who determined that she had died as a result of two severe blows to her head, which had rendered her immediately unconscious. The doctors concluded that Grace died from the combination of these severe wounds and drowning and that the wounds were consistent with blows from a tennis racket.

The boathouse at the Glenmore Hotel in 1906.

Chester was found two days later at a hotel on Fourth Lake and arrested for Grace's murder. He had walked six miles south from Big Moose to Eagle Bay without reporting her death. He checked into a hotel under his real name and thereafter appeared to be a carefree tourist—canoeing, hiking and trading stories with fellow guests. He even managed to meet the Cortland women he had met on the train from DeRuyter and made plans to visit them at their camp.

The Herkimer County district attorney, George Ward, gathered an overwhelming amount of circumstantial evidence against Chester, including the use of false names on the hotel registers to hide his identity; his burial of the tennis racket, the alleged murder weapon, during his walk to Eagle Bay; his initial denials of Grace's death; and his subsequent contradictory explanations of how she fell into the lake. However, the most damaging evidence against Chester were the heartfelt letters Grace had written to him from South Otselic, which Ward read into evidence as "a voice from the grave."

Chester testified in his own defense, claiming that Grace—who could not swim—had suddenly decided to commit suicide by jumping overboard when he suggested they return to her parents and reveal her pregnancy. Chester never explained why he had failed to report her death and traveled around so breezily thereafter. Furthermore, no reasonable explanation was ever offered by the defense to explain the deep wounds on Grace's head that caused her death.

Newspaper reporters flocked to Herkimer to cover the trial, which became a nationwide sensation. On December 4, 1906, after only a few hours of deliberation, the jury returned a verdict of guilty of murder in the first degree. The mandatory sentence of death by electrocution was passed on Chester a few days later, and he was transported to the Auburn prison to await execution. His appeal to the state's highest court was denied, as were two appeals to Governor Charles Evan Hughes for clemency. Chester Gillette was executed in the electric chair at Auburn State Prison on March 30, 1908, and buried in an unmarked grave at Soule Cemetery a few miles outside Auburn.

In 1925, Theodore Dreiser wrote his classic novel *An American Tragedy* based on the Gillette-Brown case. Two movies (including *A Place in the Sun* in 1951) and an opera also derived inspiration from the case. In 2006, the diary that Chester kept during his stay at Auburn was discovered. The final entries of the diary—including an entry a few minutes before his execution—indicated that Chester had accepted his fate and the strong Christian beliefs his Salvation Army parents had long hoped he would share.

Chester's spiritual advisors indicated that he made a confession on the night before his execution but swore them to secrecy as to the details. Accordingly, the exact nature of that confession, and the true story of what happened on that rowboat in Big Moose Lake on July 11, 1906, will never be known.

Jack Sherman wrote and directed The People v. Gillette, *a play based on the Gillette murder trial, and was editor for* The Prison Diary and Letters of Chester Gillette. *He also wrote and performed in the play* Roxy, *based on the Roxalana Druse murder case and which was performed at Ilion Little Theatre in 2015.*

A ROCKY MARRIAGE ENDS IN AN AXE BLOW

By Caryl and James Hopson

Martin and Lizzie shared a passion for each other that wasn't always… loving. They grew up as neighbors in the rural Herkimer County community of Dutchtown in the town of Salisbury. The 1904 marriage of Martin Fynn and Elizabeth Doxtater was preceded, a short time before, by a huge row. Elizabeth (Lizzie) and her mother attempted to stop Martin from entering their property by hitting him over the head with a flower stand and metal cans. It is from this violent encounter that love apparently blossomed, as they were married just a short time later. This was not a union made in heaven, as facts were soon to bear out.

Life was not easy for the good folk who resided in this region of rolling hills and sandy loam. For Lizzie, this was not her first marriage. She had previously married Fred Near on February 22, 1888, in Stratford. They had a daughter they named Lulu in 1891, but sadly, their young girl did not live out the year. After that, her husband had strayed twice, and Lizzie and Fred divorced in 1899 when she returned to Dutchtown to live with her parents, Horace and Elizabeth Metz Doxtater.

It was shortly after this time that Lizzie developed a relationship with her neighbor, Martin Fynn. They had been schoolmates, but a seven-year difference in age kept them from being little more than acquaintances in these earlier years. That was to change after Lizzie's divorce from Fred.

There had been problems between the Fynns and Doxtaters centered on a property dispute on adjoining lands. Despite this issue, young Lizzie and Martin developed an on-again, off-again love. In mid-1904, Martin called on the Doxtater household in a less than loving frame of mind. According to an article in the *Little Falls Evening Times* newspaper, Lizzie and her mother claimed that Martin intruded on their residence, attempting to choke them. They responded by throwing a fusillade of objects—"mustard cans and flower pots"—at Martin. The flower stand landed squarely on his head. Charges and countercharges were brought, but all were dismissed in a court of law.

Incredibly, their love continued, and the pair were wed on November 9 at the Methodist parsonage in Salisbury, just a few short weeks after this fiery encounter. Their marriage would continue in this vein of discord, with a series of quarrels and separations followed by happy reunions and short stints of living together again. It was during one of these breakups that

Cemetery markers for Lizzie Doxtater and Martin Fynn.

Lizzie had pleaded with Martin to return to their home on a warm summer day on June 18, 1908. This would be their last reconciliation. Unbeknownst to Lizzy, Martin had reached the end of the line. He decided to leave her and, to that end, took Lizzy to an attorney's office in Dolgeville to talk about arranging a settlement of support.

After the fateful meeting with the barrister, Martin and Lizzie returned home together one last time. That evening, as Martin lay asleep in their bed, Lizzie went to the barn, retrieved a double-bladed axe, came back to the room and struck him once on the left side of the neck, severing the jugular vein. She sat by the bedside and watched her husband die. Overcome with what she had just done, she took some morphine. Was this the same morphine she had possibly given to her husband to sleep so soundly? According to the *Rome Daily Sentinel* newspaper, found next to the bed where he bled to death was half a glass of lemonade on the nightstand. Was this how Lizzy was able to commit her grisly act? Apparently, the newspaper writer thought so, but that fact was never established by police investigators.

Lizzie then ran a quarter of a mile to her parents' home, where she told of her deed to her shocked mother and father. She confessed to her mother that "she could not live without Finn [*sic*] and was not going to let him live without her," according to the *Utica Herald Dispatch*.

The Doxtaters immediately went for medical help, and Lizzie ran back to her home. Distraught, with the morphine not having the effect she had wanted, she went to the barn, found a bottle of Paris Green insecticide and swallowed its contents. She then went back to the house, where her husband lay dead.

By the time Dr. Wood of Salisbury arrived, accompanied by Lizzie's parents, she was unconscious. Wood tried to revive her for several hours, but she succumbed to the poison. Lizzie and Martin now both lie at the Dibble-Tuttle Cemetery in Salisbury, but in different locations, their "can't live with, can't live without" relationship to continue through eternity.

MURDER ON GARDEN STREET

By Angela Harris

The little stone building at 535 Garden Street in Little Falls seems a bit out of place, surrounded as it is by grander houses. But its dark exterior suggests some of the darkness in its past. On March 5, 1915, that one-story building was the site of a lurid crime scene: the murder of Anna Malriak by Mike Malriak, her husband. The Malriaks had been married for six years when neighbor Alex Mack of 512 Garden Street was woken up at about 3:00 a.m. by Mr. Malriak, who arrived at his door in his bloody nightclothes. Malriak had walked down the street without shoes, leaving bloody footprints between the two houses. He was wearing an undershirt, the sleeves and front of which were covered with blood and, according to some reports, kerosene.

Malriak told his neighbor about a terrible fight that had taken place with his wife earlier in the night. He claimed that he needed help, as his wife was planning to set fire to the house. Malriak claimed that he and his wife had spent an evening in heated conversation after he returned from a trip to Tarrytown, where he had gone looking for work. His quest unsuccessful, he said that his wife was angry at him for being out of work and for spending money when he was not earning any.

Mack brought Malriak into his house and left him there as he hurried to the police department to report what he knew of the crime. Captain Dundon is said to have expected evidence of a domestic struggle of "average strenuosity" as he returned with Mack to the little stone house, but the men did not expect to find a murder victim. Malriak's apartment was on the east side of the building, and on the left was John O'Loughlin's store. Upon

The Malriak home. *Courtesy of Little Falls Historical Society.*

discovering the front door unlocked, they entered to find a smoky room, filled with the stench of burning kerosene and flesh. The outer door opened directly into the kitchen, and with the aid of a search light, Dundon was able to find the burned body of Anna Malriak, lying in a pool of blood on the kitchen floor. Much of her clothing had burned from her body except for the stockings she had apparently worn to bed. Charred remains of the rest of her clothes surrounded her body on the floor. Her torso was covered with burns and blisters, and she had apparently been struck on the head.

The small apartment had clearly been the scene of a violent altercation, with furniture and kitchenware strewn about. The bedding was bloody and the walls spattered with blood. A poignant symbol of better times, a Christmas bell, was hanging from the kitchen ceiling.

Dundon returned to the Mack residence, where he arrested Michael Malriak. Officer Noonan took the suspect to booking, while the investigation was handled by Dundon, Noonan and Officer Buckley of the Little Falls Police Department. After the initial work, Captain Long took up the case. Coroner McGillicudy was summoned after the discovery of the body; he ordered that the remains be removed directly to the Dineen undertaking parlor. They posited that the woman had been dead for some time since rigor mortis had set in before the police arrived. The autopsy was performed by Drs. H.W. Vickers and W.E. Hess. The doctors determined that the blow to the victim's head was the source of the pool of blood but had not caused her death. They found no evidence of skull fracture. Rather, the attributed her death to the burns from kerosene and inhalation of toxic fumes.

Late in the day of the murder's discovery, Chief Long and Captain Dundon accompanied District Attorney Farrell to the Malriak home to view the scene of the crime. At 6:15 p.m. on the evening of March 5, Malriak was arraigned for murder in the first degree before Recorder Collins. The accused was Hungarian by birth and apparently had some trouble with English, so he was provided with an interpreter named Henry Alpert. The accused's statement was recorded by the stenographer, Mr. Burnes:

> *I am 35 years old. On my way home last night I drank two spring waters and two beers. When I got home I made a fire in the stove and then I waited for my wife to come home. I got supper and we ate it together. We sat in the house talking until about 11 o'clock and then went to bed together. She was telling me I spend too much money and I told her she spent too much money. This conversation took place while we were in bed, before we went to sleep....* [Malriak described being awakened by his wife and having an argument about clocks.] *Then she said she was going to holler. She got out of bed and struck me with a poker. I don't know where she got it. She struck me on the forehead, over the left eye, and I then struck her in the mouth. I then chased her around the table.*

The prisoner denied that he had killed his wife, that she did not fall to the floor when he struck her. He also denied that he threw kerosene oil on her and blamed the fire on his wife, saying that she was trying to set the house on fire. He admitted to being jealous of his wife and wanting to move away from the neighborhood.

Malriak's statements about the crime varied over the first day, including at one point the assertion that she had poured the kerosene on herself, but District Attorney Farrell spoke for the people, while the accused stated that he did not desire to have anyone represent him. He was held for the grand jury in June. Officer McLaughlin took him to the Herkimer jail on the trolley at about 7:00 p.m.

Before the case could be brought to the grand jury, reports led the coroner to have Malriak examined by Drs. Eveleth and Santry of Little Falls to determine if he was sane. On March 19, 1915, the doctors and assorted witnesses were called to review the sanity of the accused. At least one man who was jailed at the same time, John F. Smith, as well as Sheriff Stitt and Turnkey Decker, who observed him at the Herkimer jail, reported that his "cries and groans" made the jail and surroundings "hideous." The doctors determined that he was "insane." The opinion of the doctors was supported by testimony from Chief Long of Little Falls and reports from "many friends" who said he had been acting "peculiarly" for several weeks before the murder. On the basis of this judgment, Malriak was to be committed to the asylum of the criminal insane at Matteawan near Beacon, New York, and transported to the asylum by Sheriff Stitt and Deputy Waterbury.

The story of the crime, the killer and the victim is not unusual. And the details of their lives are limited, but a few are known. Anna Malriak had been born Anna Janilk, and she had apparently grown up near Germantown, where her family still lived at the time of her death. Her brother, who sold eggs from the farm, traveled to Little Falls to make funeral arrangements after her death. She was taken to Wilcox cemetery from the Dineen undertaking rooms, with Reverend Mr. Putra of the Slovak church officiating. The brother sold whatever goods were in the Garden Street house and returned home.

It's not clear how the Malriaks made their way to Little Falls, but records show that the couple were married in Yonkers. Anna Malriak was described as a woman of slight build who worked at the Gilbert Mill at the time of her death. She was also reported to have been active with the Industrial Workers of the World (IWW) in the Little Falls Textile Strike of 1912.

Mike Malriak was out of work at the time of the crime, and on several occasions, he said that his wife berated him for this. He reported his joblessness as the impetus for the fight that ended in his wife's death. His last known employment was at Barnet Leather in Little Falls. Even so, investigators focused on jealousy and the "insanity" of the murderer, having dismissed money as a source for the argument, in spite of some of his statements. As evidence for this, they focused on the fact that, when arrested, Mike Malriak had forty-three dollars on him. Anna Malriak, the deceased, was found to have had ninety-one dollars rolled up in her stocking. Neither the stockings nor the money was burned.

CAUGHT ON FILM

By Caryl Hopson

It was Oscar Whitehead's dream to make it to Hollywood one day as an actor and be on the big screen. What he didn't realize was that the fruition of his dream would be his undoing.

On April 9, 1917, he returned to Herkimer in the custody of Sheriff James W. Moon from Los Angeles, California, on a train; he was speedily swept away in a car and taken to the Herkimer County Jail. His charge: kidnapping his younger half sister, Helen Burns Whitehead, almost three and a half years earlier.

Oscar R. Whitehead was born on November 30, 1871, the son of William H. and Florence Helmer Whitehead. His father was a well-known and respected personage in Herkimer, one of Herkimer's prominent mercantile enterprises on Main Street, the W.H. Whitehead Drug Company (later becoming the Gallinger Drug Company). His mother died when he was twelve, and his father remarried two more times. His second marriage was to Fanny Gloo in 1885, and at that time, Oscar entered Albany Medical College to take a course in pharmacy. But following in his father's footsteps was not to be—he quit and took a job with the Metropolitan Insurance Company. This, too, was a short-lived experience when he was let go after it was discovered he was forging policies in order to collect additional money. He drifted from job to job and even became an actor for a brief time. He had taken to drink and consorted with women with less than respectable reputations, all while living at home with his father and stepmother, leading to family quarrels. When he finally entered Fairfield Military Academy to study stenography, this was his chance to get his life straightened out, but once again, it was not to be. He was dismissed for "intoxication and ungentlemanly conduct." Oscar had obtained employment with the Standard Furniture Company and continued to drink until he had found something that would change his life: religion. Christian Science was just emerging at the end of the nineteenth century, and people were drawn to its practice of spiritual healing and the promise of renewed faith. Oscar changed his habits and became a model citizen, although his peculiarities still gave him the label of "eccentric" by his family and acquaintances. He was a square peg in the round hole of life in the community of Herkimer.

In 1900, William Whitehead married his third wife, Margaret (Madge) Burns, with whom he had three daughters, Margaret and twins Ruth and

Oscar Whitehead as portrayed in the newspapers at the time he escaped to California with his younger sister Helen.

Helen. Oscar lived with his new stepfamily at 506 Church Street in Herkimer. He had steady employment at the Standard Furniture Company as a bookkeeper, was an active member with the local Masons and helped organize the Herkimer Esperanto Club, a movement to create a unifying world language that had started in 1880s in eastern Europe. It did not have a large following but proved that Oscar was drawn to new and atypical movements and that he had an intelligent mind. He wrote extensively and submitted some of his work to publishers, but it had been refused.

Oscar dearly loved his little sisters, and it was said that he developed an especially strong attachment to Helen in 1907, when she turned five. It is possible that his affection resulted from the family's earlier bereavement in losing Casper, the five-year-old son of William and Fanny, to pneumonia. He spent a lot of time with Helen, even accompanying her to and from school and instructing her on her conduct. This appeared strange to the neighbors and put him in conflict with his own father and stepmother on occasions. He had expressed a desire to take her to New York City on a visit in 1911 but was discouraged by the parents.

It was nearing the holiday of Thanksgiving 1913, and Oscar had resigned his position at the Standard Furniture Company and was off to New York City to sell his automobile. He had expressed a desire to go on a trip to Los Angeles, California, and once again asked if he could take Helen; again he was refused. At this time, he was age forty-two and she was nearing eleven. After conducting his business in the city, he traveled by train to Syracuse, bypassing Herkimer. What was not known to the family was that the two siblings had conspired for Helen to meet Oscar there on Thanksgiving Day. Helen had complained about a toothache that morning and went to be treated by a dentist, going on her own and reassuring her parents that she would be back in time for them to go to Ilion, where they would spend the day with Mrs. Whitehead's mother. When she didn't appear by the appointed time, they became worried and began looking for her, eventually enlisting the support of local residents and the local authorities. The fire bell was sounded, and people gathered at the Municipal Building. County Judge

Bell addressed them, initiating a search throughout the village from house to house; a bloodhound named "General Lee" was even brought in from Oneida. He led the search party to the trolley station.

The next day, Mrs. Whitehead received a letter from Helen herself. In it, she stated, "My dear Mother: I couldn't stand it without Oscar and I am going to Los Angeles with him. Don't worry about me. When Oscar gets a position we'll send for you. Will write you often and you write me. I will write you first and give you my address. I am under good care. Lovingly your daughter, Helen Whitehead." She had also enclosed instructions that Oscar had given her to meet him in Syracuse, and he had enclosed two dollars "in case anything should have gone wrong with the money she had hidden in the toe of her shoe."

Mr. Whitehead released a statement of these facts and was not initially alarmed, stating that they would bring them back and "he was confident that no harm will befall the girl." The headlines read, "Unbalanced Brother Abducts Sister" and "Actor Runs Away with Half Sister." The chase to find the missing girl and her older brother was on, involving the New York police, detective agencies and the Masons. Through the local Herkimer Lodge, the Grand Master of New York State reached out to all the lodges in the country to be on the lookout for the pair, issuing photographs and circulars with a detailed description. No trace was found.

Helen Whitehead around age eleven.

It was months before they heard from Oscar in a letter to his father on February 10, 1914, postmarked Paris; he reassured his father that Helen was well cared for and that he had obtained a good job in Paris, but authorities there could not locate them even after a thorough investigation. It was later discovered that Oscar had asked an acquaintance working for Standard Furniture Company based in Paris to mail it for him.

It would be three years later that a fluke moment would do what years of searching by professionals couldn't do in finding Oscar Whitehead. It took place at a motion picture show at Herkimer. A volunteer at the Herkimer County Historical Society, Tod Waterbury, told us the tale years ago. His version was that as the movie played, someone in the audience yelled out, "That's Oscar Whitehead in the background!" The police were called, and the theater ran the movie for them and, presumably, the girl's parents. The motion picture company was contacted, as were the police in California.

After a two-week search, the pair were located living in apartments at 2007 Argyle Avenue under the names H. (Horace) O. Perline and Susie Perline. Sheriff Moon, along with Mrs. Whitehead and Reverend Brinckerhoff, went to California to retrieve them. It was learned that Helen had been attending a private school, while Oscar worked for film companies. Oscar maintained that "he developed the child Helen into one of the most spiritual and moral girls in the world and that in no way has he harmed the child."

He arrived back in Herkimer with a changed appearance—a full beard and long hair—as well as the threat of indictment for child abduction looming before him. But public sympathy was on his side. The *Herkimer Citizen* wrote, "If Oscar Whitehead has acted only as a father to Helen, and treated her kindly, he should in my opinion be sent to a sanitarium where the weak minded are cared for." Drs. Harold Palmer and George Campbell from the State Hospital at Utica examined him at the Herkimer County Jail and in their opinion deemed him insane, noting that he should be committed based on his appearance, for one. "He wears his hair long, tied at the back with a string. His beard also is long and untrimmed." The '70s would have shocked these doctors.

On May 2, 1917, County Judge Charles Bell ordered that Oscar be removed and committed to Matteawan State Hospital, where "he shall remain until restored to his right mind." While there, Oscar made repeated attempts to be released from the institution in hearings he obtained through habeas corpus, for which he was brought back to Herkimer, but was denied. One of the times in May 1918, on his seventh attempt at liberty through the courts, he took matters into his own hands while being returned to Matteawan. He escaped out a car window on the train and wasn't found until the next day at a nearby farm, where he had procured employment. Finally, in 1924, the superintendent of the asylum, Dr. R.F.C. Kieb, stated to the court that "Whitehead had shown improvement since being committed to the asylum and if friends could be found who would take him and be responsible for his acts he would be willing to sanction his

Photographs of the pair from local newspapers when they were brought back from California.

release." On January 30, the county judge of Herkimer County ordered the discharge of Oscar for deportation to California. The indictment for kidnapping had not been dismissed, and the threat of it being reinstituted was most likely to keep him from returning to New York.

Oscar returned to his life in California in the motion picture industry, as can be seen in the 1930 census, which shows he was living as a lodger at 758½ El Centro Avenue in Hollywood, with his occupation listed as "actor." He resumed the name of H.O. Perline, which could be a stage name. We do not know if he tried to communicate with his family. He died on August 13, 1941, in California.

Helen, from newspaper accounts, was glad to be home with her family. She graduated from Herkimer High School and married Carl B. Lundstrom on October 20, 1923. They had two sons, C. William and David. Carl was associated with his father in the operation of the C.J. Lundstrom Manufacturing Company in Little Falls and would later found Lundstrom Laboratories. He died of a heart attack at the age of fifty-six in the year 1956, and Helen took over the responsibility of running the company with her eldest son, Carl. She died on November 24, 1997, at the age of ninety-four.

A MURDER OF FORGIVENESS

By Dennis Webster

Jean Gianini hit teacher Lida Beecher on the back of the head with a rusty monkey wrench with such force that her glasses flew off several feet onto the fresh snow. She dropped her umbrella, fell to her hands and knees and clutched the snow as she struggled to remain alive. A few more wrench blows to the head left her still conscious but groaning as the sixteen-year-old student took out the butcher knife he had in his coat pocket and ended her life with several savage stabs. She was twenty-one years old. Her crimson blood seeped out onto the pure white snow. The shocking crime took place on March 27, 1914, on Buck Hill Road in the village of Poland, New York, a close-knit small town of 350 in the town of Russia and Herkimer County. Jean Gianini's murder of Lida Beecher would result in a trial and verdict that few would believe and still resonates in Herkimer County to this day.

Jean Gianini was born in the Bronx, New York, where his father ran a successful furniture business. Jean was rejected by his mother at birth. Sally Gianini had refused to hold him. She would be committed to an insane asylum and pass away, never giving love to her son. Jean was unable to walk and talk until he was five years old and struggled with getting along with other children. He was called "looney" and had been prone to lashing out; once he was discovered eating mud pies while being egged on by older boys. Charles Gianini met and married a woman from the town of Russia and moved his family to Poland so Jean could get a fresh start. Jean had physical issues along with his mental struggles and would be small at five-foot-three and walked with a gait.

His behavior never improved, as he was prone to run away and jump trains, and he was described as odd and different by the children of the village. Jean had been a student of Lydia "Lida" Beecher at Poland School and had fallen behind his younger peers. He had been restless in the classroom and had been disciplined for his odd mannerisms. Lida tried to help Jean and wrote letters of support to get him in other schools that could help him. She spoke to Jean's father about what was going on, as she cared for her student. This proved to be a fatal decision, as Jean felt Lida was out to get him. She ratted him out. Jean would have to leave Poland School for bad behavior and was sent away to a reform school in Utica, New York, where he had to scrub laundry for months until he was released. He would return to Poland an angry young man. He would get his revenge.

Lida Beecher (*center*), with friends Ethel Plum (*left*) and Florence Schermerhorn (*front*) in Poland. *Courtesy of Paula Johnson, town of Russia historian.*

Lida Beecher was a young woman whose tenure at Poland School District was her first after graduating from Cortland Normal School. She was a devout Christian and taught religious classes while living in Poland. She lived in a home almost across the street from Jean in the middle of the village. Lida made friends easily, as she was personable, sweet and attractive. She had her entire life ahead of her to teach and inspire.

After Jean killed Lida, he threw away the monkey wrench, put the butcher knife in his jacket pocket and ran back down Buck Hill Road. He wiped the blood off the knife, put it back in his family's kitchen drawer and went to bed. At 8:00 a.m. the following morning, a farmer, Henry Fitch, came upon a streak of blood across the road. He got out, and at the spot of the murder, he found Lida's glasses, umbrella and a broken hair clip. There was a blood streak two hundred yards in length, as Jean later confessed to grabbing Lida by the ankle and dragging her across the road, hiding her body under a thicket. Jean woke up and walked the railroad tracks down to Newport, the village next door to Poland. There had been witnesses who had seen Jean walking with Lida down Main Street and up Buck Hill Road. The boy was careless and had even tried to solicit friends to try to kill Lida. His anger at her was well known, and now the police were looking for him. Within hours, he was picked up by the sheriff and readily and happily confessed to the crime, saying with a smile, "I got my revenge." Jean signed a confession and was arrested and taken to the Herkimer County Courthouse in Herkimer, where he resided in the same jail cell that had held the executed murderer Chester Gillette.

Jean's criminal trial was a circus, with thousands of onlookers, supporters and a throng of curious young women. The most expensive trial in the history of Herkimer County, it brought a packed train from Poland every day that had family and friends. The case garnered front-page headlines across the country and attracted the world's best alienists, who would play vital roles in the outcome. The prosecution was led by the brilliant Herkimer County district attorney Charles Thomas. Jean's father spent his life savings in order to hire the high-powered New York City defense attorney John McIntyre. Overseeing the trial was Judge Irving Devendorf, who had previously worked on the Chester Gillette murder trial that resulted in Chester being fried in the electric chair in Auburn, New York. Jean's trial could've seen the same results, as the sixteen-year-old was charged with first-degree murder.

In the front row was Jean's father, Charles, and his sister, Moffie. Lida's father, Reverend Dr. William Beecher, was on the other side, carefully watching the proceedings. The preacher had paid a visit to Jean in his cell before the trial and never revealed what the two had discussed. Jean's confession was a powerful piece of evidence, and the defense never disagreed with it, as it was going for a not guilty verdict by reason of insanity. Jean spent the trial restless, picking his fingernails, yawning and acting peculiar. The prosecution used that as him being a coldblooded murderer with no remorse. The twelve jurors were put to the test, but the testimony of the world's leading expert on "imbeciles," Dr. Henry H. Goddard, was the key to the shocking verdict. Dr. Goddard had seen more than forty thousand imbeciles in his storied eighteen-year career and would apply the Binet test to Jean. Alfred Binet (1857–1911) had invented the mental test and used it in France. Jean's trial was the first in the history of the United States where the

Photograph of Jean Gianini after he was taken to the Herkimer County Jail.

Charles Gianini, the father of Jean.

Binet test was allowed. The test asked very basic questions, and the result gives the mental age of the person. Jean was sixteen physically, but the test determined that he had the mental abilities of a ten-year-old. Dr. Goddard deemed him a "high grade imbecile." Dr. A. Walter Suiter, whose medical office was right next door to the courthouse, was a highly respected physician and well known in Herkimer County. Dr. Suiter examined Jean and came back with the same determination as Dr. Goddard. Charles Thomas would fight these opinions with great vigor, as Jean showed intelligence in his mannerisms. Thomas stated that Jean was aware of what he was doing, relished in the murder and signed a confession with a grin on his face. The defense put Jean's father on the stand, and Charles Gianini talked about Jean's mother and his son's struggles mentally and physically. Charles said that he didn't think his son deserved to be executed but that he should never be free and would be better served being placed in a mental health care facility. Jean felt he was doomed to the electric chair and never expected the verdict.

The jurors had more than four thousand pages of typed court transcripts to review as they recessed to make their decision. The trial had been emotionally charged, with both sides fighting and presenting stellar cases. The major opinion at the time was that Jean would be put to death in the electric chair, but the testimonies of Charles Gianini, Dr. Goddard and Dr. Suiter swung the jury; the men came back with the verdict of not guilty by reason of insanity. There was outrage in the courtroom and in the press. Many felt that the jurors had been fooled and under the spell of defense attorney McIntyre. But reading through the court transcripts, it becomes clear that Jean was seriously mentally ill. Modern psychiatrists state that Jean would be diagnosed as having autism, but because he was high functioning, he'd be considered to have autism spectrum disorder. Jean's case was so unique that Dr. Goddard wrote a book after the case called *The Criminal Imbecile*, in which Jean is prominently featured.

Jean's life would not be easy, as he was brought to Matteawan State Hospital for the Criminally Insane in Dutchess County, New York. Outrage in the press was further inflated when the guards at the Herkimer County Jail released a poem Jean had written and left in his cell. The newspapers printed this shocking poem:

JEAN'S JAILHOUSE POEM

My name is Gianini I would have you know.
And I always have trouble wherever I go.
To be thought a tough it is my delight.
And I'm thinking and planning both day and night.
I killed Lida Beecher with an old monkey wrench.
And they took me before the judge on the bench.
The sentence they gave me it caused me to smile.
It was "He is not guilty he's an imbecile."
Now here is thanks to the jurors who let me go free.
The foolishest men I ever did see.
When they came marching in it raised up my hair.
I thought sure they'd say "He must sit in the chair."
Now, soon I must leave you and bid adieu.
And the dollars I've cost you won't be a few.
I never will fear if I can find McIntyre.
For I really believe he could save me from hell-fire.

—Jean Martinette Gianini

Could the father of a murdered daughter forgive the killer? Lida's father, Reverend Dr. William A. Beecher, was a man of deep faith. He was the preacher at a small church in Sennett, New York. He came to Herkimer to retrieve his daughter's body and bring it back home for burial and funeral services. Reverend Beecher went to the Herkimer County Jail and visited Jean. The reverend walked up and said, "I am the father of Lida Beecher. I thought you might want to speak with me. I have but a few minutes to speak with you but I wanted to know how you got her up that hill." Jean was open to the preacher coming into his jail cell. The conversation was private and the reverend would not discuss the content, but he did say he forgave Jean for his crime.

People were astounded at this soft-spoken, white-haired country preacher forgiving the boy who had murdered his daughter. The *New York Tribune* sent a sociological worker from the city to interview the gentle man to see how he could forgive such a crime. Boyd Fisher took to train to the town of Sennett, where he sat in the kitchen of Reverend Beecher's house and chatted about the crime, forgiveness and the vice of the young. Fisher asked what was discussed when the reverend visited Jean in his cell, and Reverend Beecher responded, "The boy has told me some things about how he murdered my daughter which he has told no one else and which is regarded as confidential. Unless he chooses to tell publicly all he knows, I shall not violate his confidences." Fisher was astonished that Reverend Beecher had forgiven Jean and showed him "bitter pity."

It was widely known that Lida had helped her pupil on other occasions and had been murdered at a time when she was again assisting the boy. Fisher described that when he was in Herkimer, citizens were whispering that the boy should be lynched, yet Reverend Beecher was forgiving. Fisher was amazed that Reverend Beecher could keep hate for Jean out of his Christian heart. Reverend Beecher said that he loved Jean: "Lida died as I would have her die. In the performance of her duty. She was betrayed and crucified, like the master, by those whom she served. I am sure some great good will come of it." Reverend Beecher used the phrase "the heroism of crime." Reverend Beecher paused, looked down at his kitchen table and muttered in a low voice, "My daughter's death teaches its own lesson." The reverend said that hundreds of people had written him prayers to offer God's grace to sustain him. The kind preacher then said to Fisher, "My daughter, however, was doing one more kindness to one who had often disappointed her. If she had been killed coming home from some dance or other frivolous amusement there would have been no inspiration for the world in her murder. But her death was a martyrdom such as God is continually regarding of us to save the world." Reverend Beecher paused while his lone living daughter removed dishes. Only after she had left did he go back to addressing Fisher by saying, "Lida's pastor tells me that only the night before her death she attended a prayer meeting and led the service. He said he'll never forget her heartfelt words....The boy is no different and no worse than boys right here in Sennett, and in every village and city in the country whose physical health is weakened by cigarette smoking and other vices and whose imaginations are inflamed by motion pictures of crime and by cheap novels. As I looked at the boy, I saw behind him these influences, which I have always fought, and am still fighting, and I held them, not him, chiefly responsible." In those days, a boy who smoked cigarettes was considered the worst kind of person and a true criminal.

The tragedy of this case was in the time when the murder occurred. In our modern times, Jean would have been diagnosed at an early age and given treatment that would have had him living an independent and productive life. Lida's preacher father provided Jean with a death of forgiveness. Jean would not spend the rest of his life in mental health institutions, as at an old age he was transferred to a nursing home, where he quietly and peacefully lived out the rest of his days with visits by his family. Upon his death, he was buried in an unmarked grave at St. Charles Cemetery in Farmingdale, New York, his soul finally at peace.

Dennis Webster is the author of books on true crime, ghosts and asylums. His book Murder of a Herkimer County Teacher: The 1914 Case of a Vengeful Student *is the complete and in-depth analysis of the Jean Gianini/Lida Beecher murder case and trial.*

ARTHUR W. WOOD MURDERED IN SCHUYLER

By Wendy Ladd Weeks

Arthur W. Wood never returned home for midday dinner. Working alone in the potato field between his mother's farm on Wood Road and his own homestead at Baker Corners, Arthur met with his fate. Assuming that he was lunching at his mother's, his wife waited. But when local friends came to help with the evening chores, her fears must have turned to anguish.

Just months prior to this September evening, Arthur and Della had endured pain and suffering beyond the pale for any parents. Their ten-year-old son, Glenn, had died in December from an unsuccessful operation for pancreatitis. Then in March, their eldest son, twelve-year-old Albert, had died in a freak accident. While out hunting, the gun he was holding upright in a sleigh discharged when bouncing on the floor of the sleigh. The gun blew a hole in his heart.

The moon's phase was just a slit of waxing crescent the night of Thursday, September 17, 1914, and it had not yet risen when "began the searching of the fields with lanterns, in which practically every man in Schuyler took part."[20] Then, around 11:00 p.m., Arthur's body was found with two bullet holes in his torso.

A THRICE STRICKEN FAMILY.

ARTHUR WOOD'S FAMILY, IN DECEMBER INTACT, NOW NEARLY HALF GONE.

[Man who was murdered Thursday noon near Schuyler Corners. One of the sons died in December and the other was shot in February.]

A neighbor and his son, Merritt and Almon Tanner, had heard two gunshots ring out around noon that day. They had just assumed that woodchucks were the target. They had seen a man running east in the pasture toward Thomas Davis's barn and house on Newport Road. Later, when Mr. Wood's body was found, this was the location where the suspect had been seen.

The newspaper in Little Falls first published a brief account of the murder, suggesting that it was someone stealing produce who killed Mr. Wood. The *Utica Saturday Globe* coincidentally had a brief article on its back page concerning general mobilization orders that had been sent to the farmers of Schuyler Township by the Vigilance Committee, citing "many thefts of produce in the town": "Each of the reserves is to arm himself with a shotgun and be prepared to keep constant watch on potato patches and cornfields so that the devastators thereof may be made to suffer for their pernicious activities."[21]

But in the same *Saturday Globe* newspaper, published on September 19, there is a lengthy description of the murder of Arthur Wood with no clear reasoning for the murder. "The neighbors have evolved a theory, the only one that seems tenable, that hunters scouring the woods for game, may have been asked to show their license. Mr. Wood was a constable and had a right to ask any man carrying a gun. It is presumed they had no license and to escape a $25 fine shot the officer." This theory was advanced by Sheriff Stitt, District Attorney Farrell and Coroner Huyck, who were investigating the murder. Another motive, less substantiated, is the possibility that Arthur may have had cash in his pants pocket.

The suspicion of game law violators being the murderers continued for days and weeks as more newspapers picked up the story. Another murder, of a game warden, in Rome, New York, was compared to this senseless murder. More suspicions arose, with more accounts surfacing of men fleeing the Wood murder scene appearing to be of foreign descent. "The Herkimer County authorities have made use of a blood hound belonging to Chief Keller of Frankfort, and the dog followed a trail that ended at the Mohawk river. The length of time between the shooting and the finding of the body made it difficult to trace the murderer."[22]

Now a widow, Mrs. Wood, with her remaining family of four young daughters, had to sell her farm and home. The farm was sold on October 2, just weeks after this tragedy, and all the equipment was disposed of at public auction. The family moved in with Arthur's mother on Herkimer Road. The sheriff and coroner's department continued "vigorously prosecuting the search of the slayer since the day Wood's body was found in a field near his home, but have found no clue."[23]

Prior to the sale of Wood's home, services were conducted there. Hundreds came to pay their respects to the family of the man whose murder is still a mystery. As written in the *Utica Daily Press* on the morning of September 21, 1914, "Seldom has a funeral in that locality been so largely attended, sympathy aroused through the peculiarly sad affliction of this family having drawn many who had little more than a casual acquaintance with Mr. Wood. All united however, in deploring his unfortunate death and in hoping for his bereaved relatives that consolation which alone can temper grief as theirs."[24]

Mr. Arthur Wood, forty-one, was buried at the West Schuyler Cemetery on Newport Road in Schuyler, a quick walk from where his lifeless body was found. The Wood homestead was located on the northeast side of the Cosby Manor Road and Newport Road intersection. Mr. Merritt Tanner's home is the brick house once owned by Cogar Corporation on Cosby Manor Road and is now being renovated, and it is from there where the murder site could be seen in a clear, unobstructed view looking south in the field just east of the current VFW on Wood Road. Thomas E. Davis's barn still stands in the backyard of the Durr residence on Newport Road—Arthur Wood's body was found within two hundred yards of the barn.

Like the last breath of a soul disappearing into the ether of time, a whisper of a recap of the murder was logged on January 1, 1915, in the *Utica Daily Press*: "It was the theory of the officers that Wood had been killed by some foreigners who were violating the game laws. His murderer has never been apprehended."

THE NOTORIOUS 1916 LITTLE FALLS TRUNK MURDER

By Jeffrey Gressler

On January 2, 1917, Little Falls resident Michael Masco pleaded guilty to second-degree murder and received a sentence of twenty years of hard labor at Auburn. His wife, Elizabeth, pleaded guilty to manslaughter for the same crime. She received a sentence of three years and five months. Who was murdered and what were the circumstances that led to these arrests and convictions?

This story begins on November 4, 1916, when a group of young boys made a grisly discovery in a dump that once sat alongside Southern Avenue south of the Mohawk River in the city of Little Falls. Curiosity led the boys to open a partially buried trunk to find a dismembered body. Terrified, the boys ran to a canal workman, who in turn alerted the police.

It was eventually determined that the unfortunate victim was Rosolini Ciprotti, aged thirty-nine, but it took a lot of good detective work to unravel the mystery of what has become known as the most notorious murder in Little Falls history.

According to fellow rooming house boarder Guiseppe Dagostino, Ciprotti had "been visiting a woman" at her home mornings after her husband departed for work. That woman was Elizabeth Masco.

Mike Masco got tipped off about his wife's tryst and spied from a building across the street one morning after he had supposedly left for work. Masco spotted Ciprotti and then took action. He crossed the street with gun in pocket and malice in his heart.

Masco quietly entered his house, where he surprised the embracing pair and then he shot and killed Ciprotti. His wife begged him not to shoot her. Masco instead compelled her to assist him by hiding the body in the basement before reporting late for work—the latter led, in part, to his undoing.

That evening, the Mascos performed the grisly task of dismembering Ciprotti's body so that it would fit into a hauling trunk. Masco next transported the trunk by wheelbarrow from his 85 Mohawk Street home over a bridge spanning the Erie Canal and then along Southern Avenue to the dumping area, where he hid the trunk under a mass of wild grapevines, where it awaited discovery by the young boys. The Mascos then returned to their basement to clean up, but they did not do quite a good enough job.

Before there could be any arrests, trials or convictions, the facts of the case had to be uncovered. Enter Little Falls police chief James "Dusty" Long, Captain John Dundon and Officer Noonan. Long carefully studied the dump and surrounding fields where the body had been discovered and determined that there were no heavy tire tracks. Long deduced, "Since no one saw the killer, that means that he did not have to travel very far. And that takes me right into the block of houses at the edge of the field. That is where the victim lived, and that's where I will find the man who murdered him." Events would prove him correct.

Meanwhile, the victim needed to be identified. The corpse was painstakingly "reassembled" and laid out at Dineen's funeral home. Upon invitation, many city residents walked past the body, but no one was able to identify the victim.

Long then went from house to house in the neighborhood nearby the field trying to determine if someone was missing. Eventually, he came upon Therda Ciani, who owned the boardinghouse where Ciprotti lived. She told Long that Ciprotti had been missing for some time. Interestingly, Ciprotti had also once boarded in the Masco home.

At first, Ciani refused to view the body, but Long threatened to arrest her if she did not cooperate. Upon viewing the body, the woman burst into horrified screams before reluctantly providing the police with positive identification. Having identified the victim, the police set out to find the murderer. Long searched for a handcart or wheelbarrow in the nearby neighborhoods. He located one in a Mohawk Street backyard, where he saw fresh sand in its bottom; upon scraping it away, he found bloodstains. He then theorized that the murder must have been committed in a nearby house.

Acting on a tip from Therda Ciani, Long began searching for Ciprotti's boardinghouse roommate Guiseppe Dagostino, whom he at first thought was the likely murderer. Long soon found a drunken Dagostino in a nearby barroom, where he began questioning the man. Long next brought him to police headquarters to further question the sodden suspect. Unconvinced that Dagostino was the murderer, Long locked him up on suspicion.

Long then went door to door along Mohawk Street. Eventually, he gained access to the house close by where he had found the wheelbarrow. He discovered bloodstains both in a doorway and in the basement, where he also discovered a butcher knife, a handgun and a crosscut saw with blood and hair in its teeth. The chief pressed on.

In an upstairs room, the police found additional evidence, including bullet holes in a wall and more bloodstains. Mrs. Masco was brought in for questioning. The mother of four children broke under pressure and confessed about her role in the grisly events. She told the police that her husband worked at the Barnet Leather Company on East Mill Street.

Photo at Little Falls Historical Society entitled "Trunk Murder." Could this be the trunk used to conceal this dastardly deed? *Courtesy of Little Falls Historical Society.*

Long went to the factory and asked to see employee time cards. He discovered that Masco had reported late for work on a late October workday, even though attempts had been made to smudge out his late arrival time. The final pieces were falling into place. The police brought Masco in for questioning. The man denied both his involvement and his wife's statements, but he eventually confessed to the crime when confronted with the overwhelming evidence.

On December 16, the Mascos were indicted by a grand jury. A jury was then selected from a pool of 125 people, and the case went to trial. The Mascos' attorney was Albert M. Mills, who had defended Chester Gillette a decade earlier in the infamous "American Tragedy" trial. A single day of courtroom testimony resulted in the twin guilty verdicts. A late arrival time for work and a poorly cleaned-up murder scene proved to be the damning evidence in this trial.

The horrific details of this case have given way to a single label, Little Falls's most notorious murder. Lust, jealousy, revenge and investigative prowess were all in play in this case more than a century old—long ago but not forgotten.

The neighborhoods where the murder took place and where Ciprotti's body was discovered no longer exist. Visitors to the Little Falls Historical Society Museum can view a large 1920s aerial photograph of Little Falls that shows the entire area where these events took place.

THE KILLING OF HENRY WERNER

By Roberta Walsh

On February 22, 1921, Henry Werner was found lying in a snowy ravine five hundred feet from his Ilion home. He had serious injuries to his head and neck, and it was obvious when he was found that Werner was dead. Who killed him, where and with what weapon were questions that remained to be answered.

The prime suspect was Rutger Warder, who was taken into custody immediately. Warder had been a boarder in Henry Werner's house since November 1920. When he was questioned, he claimed that Henry Werner's wife and her mother had planned the crime but that they had

Rutger Warder. *Courtesy of Roberta Walsh.*

convinced him to actually commit the murder. From that moment on, newspapers referred to him as "the self-confessed murderer." Because his confession implicated Jennie Werner and her mother, Minnie Woodbridge, they were also arrested.

Warder's trial began on March 22, 1921. Charles B. Hane and William J. Gardinier were his court-appointed attorneys. The judge was Irving R. Devendorf, the same judge who was on the bench for the Chester Gillette trial. Jennie Werner and her mother were to be tried separately at a later time.

From the first day, Warder's trial was a combination of soap opera and three-ring circus. Crowds mobbed the courtroom to hear the testimony. The trial was front-page news. Reporters from New York City to Buffalo and beyond sat in court to provide updates so that people who couldn't attend the trial in person could keep up with the latest developments. Many of Warder's friends and neighbors thought that he was innocent of the murder. Some thought that Jennie Warner had seduced Rutger Warder to commit the murder for her. A few believed that Rutger Warder had stalked Jennie Warner, murdering her husband so he could possess her.

MRS. JENNIE WARNER.

In court, Jennie Werner testified that Warder had persuaded her husband to go rabbit hunting, killed him and then threatened to kill Jennie if she told. When he took the stand, Warder claimed that he had confessed to the murder only to save Jennie, but now that Jennie had turned against him, he would tell the truth. Warder said that only four days after he moved in, Jennie Werner told him that she had been married for eleven years and knew two months into the marriage that it had been a mistake. She made it obvious that she would like to be rid of her husband. She and her mother had made plans to poison him and shoot him but did not carry them out. The night of February 21, Jennie hit Henry with an axe in the cellar and had come to Warder's bedside to tell him that she needed him to "get rid of the body." They both carried the body out to the ravine and then shot him to disguise the axe wound.

The trial lasted almost three weeks and took some strange twists and turns. The defense lost a witness. Warder was working as a chauffeur for H.P. Brayton at the time of the murder. Brayton agreed to testify about Warder's whereabouts at given times. This was probably to establish that he was not where the prosecution said he was, but Brayton died shortly before the trial started. There were rumored to be other witnesses who were afraid to come forward.

Warder had been arrested and indicted only for the murder of Henry Werner, but Judge Devendorf was apparently unfazed when the prosecution brought in witnesses to testify about two unsolved murders in Frankfort. The prosecution introduced evidence and questioned witnesses about the November 1919 murder of traveling salesman Clarence Kelly. Warder was also questioned about the murder of night watchman Albert Dade in February 1921.

Finally, in desperation, Warder's lawyers stopped trying to convince the jury that Rutger Warder was innocent or had been beguiled by Jennie Werner and instead tried to prove that he was insane. Witnesses were called who would testify that Warder's mother had been insane and that Warder had suffered a head injury and was not responsible for his actions—for one reason or the other. Warder's trial ended on April 9, 1921, and he was found guilty of murder. The judge sentenced Rutger Warder to die in the electric chair during the week of May 16.

When the trial was over, there were still many people in the community who had serious doubts about Warder's role in the murder and were against his death sentence. Later, when a petition for clemency was presented to the governor, it included signatures from all of Warder's neighbors, many residents of Ilion and even the parents of the victim and some members of the jury that handed down the verdict. After meeting Warder, the chaplain at Sing Sing said, "He was a poor fool but I don't believe that he killed Henry Werner. We do not electrocute a man for being a poor fool."

Jennie Werner's trial began on April 29, with Charles L. Earl acting as her lawyer. Earl described her as a hardworking farmer's wife and a good mother who was uneducated and too unsophisticated to hatch a murder plot. He claimed that nothing she said when she was arrested should be admissible as evidence because she was weak with hunger, having nothing to eat during the whole day that she was being questioned. He also questioned the accuracy, insisting that Assistant District Attorney Greene only "wrote down that part of what she said which he wanted to write down." Jennie Werner sat in court through most of the trial with her daughter, Elma, on her lap. Occasionally, little Elma would reach up and pat her mother's cheek to get her attention. Sometimes she would fall asleep.

Earl's strategy was not so much to defend Jennie Werner but to put Rutger Warder on trial again. He told the jury, "Warder made his selections and then went after his game like a hunter that he was. His position in the Werner home was that of the hunter reaching out after the game which he coveted. Warder and Henry were friends in business. They hunted and worked together. We will show you that their thoughts and conversation ran along the same lines. They were Hunters of Women. That is what caused the tragedy in the Werner household." Warder was the wolf and Jennie the rabbit.

Every day of the trial, the newspapers had something interesting to report. Dr. John Hurley of Little Falls testified, as a supposedly impartial expert witness, that the blood samples collected in the cellar were not human blood, throwing doubt on Warder's version of the murder. A short time later, he took the stand again to testify as a character witness and sing the praises of Jennie Werner.

The courtroom was packed when Rutger Warder was brought back from Sing Sing to testify against Jennie Warner. Attorney Earl had few questions for him about the murder but many other questions about Warder's failed marriage, his philandering and his divorce.

When Earl called Watts Bullock, constable at the jail, to the stand, he testified that during some casual chitchat at the jail, Rutger Warder told him that he had committed the murder and that he expected to get the death penalty. Bullock also explained that the person sitting on the jury who looked exactly like him was his twin brother, Bill Bullock.

District Attorney Ward had his work cut out for him. He wanted to introduce Henry Werner's life insurance policy as evidence of motive, but Jennie's attorney objected. He finally withdrew his objection, but only on condition that Ward read to the jury not just the amount of money that Jennie would get but also every single word of the entire policy. He read aloud for forty-five minutes.

When Jennie's attorney persisted in calling an expert witness "Dr. Hamilton" over and over again, even though he was not a doctor, Assistant District Attorney Green jumped from his chair to object every single time to the point where there was laughter in the courtroom. Earl insisted to Judge Devendorf that he "couldn't help himself." The newspapers described the scene and reported that Green was a stickler for accuracy.

On May 12, Jennie Werner was found not guilty. The district attorney felt that he no longer had a case against Jennie's mother and eventually set Minnie Woodbridge free. Public opinion was quite different at the end of Jennie Werner's trial, and members of the jury were harassed as they left the courtroom. Women followed them up the street yelling, "Now it is legal to kill our husbands!"

Rutger Warder's "Notice of Appeal" was received at Sing Sing on May 14, and he was granted a stay of execution to allow time for the appeal. In June, he was in the national news when he was operated on for appendicitis; doctors said that he would be completely recovered by the time he went to the electric chair.

Warder's conviction was upheld on November 22, and his execution was rescheduled for January 25, 1923. By January 22, information about Rutger Warder, the petitions and a formal plea for commutation had been received by Governor Al Smith, and on January 24, Warder's sentence was commuted to life in prison at Sing Sing.

The governor explained his reasoning for why he was commuting Warder's sentence to life in prison: "I have no doubt about the guilt of Warder, but I have doubt about the justice of exacting from him the full penalty of the law." He went on to say that he thought in the future it might come to light that there were "other people involved as seriously, if not more so, than Warder."

THE SEATTLE STAR

Operated On for Legal Execution

* * * * * * * * *

Condemned Man May Be Saved

Newspaper photo of Warder when he was at Sing Sing Prison and operated on for appendicitis before his sentence was commuted to life in prison.

Warder served his time at Sing Sing apparently without incident, making the papers again in 1933 when the National League champion New York Giants played the prison team in an exhibition contest, and Warder pitched the last inning. He appeared again working at the Albany Medical Center, apparently having been released from Sing Sing in 1948. He was hired as night receptionist at Memorial Hospital in Albany in 1953 and worked there until his death on October 27, 1963.

Jennie Werner remarried on June 2, 1923, to Leroy Hills of Utica. She died in 1981. Her mother, Minnie Woodbridge, also remarried, becoming Mrs. Frank E. Falsen. She died in 1961 at the age of ninety-four.

LURED TO THEIR DEATHS: THE MULKOON AFFAIR

By James Greiner

Louis Mulkoon and his wife, Sadie, emigrated from the Syria-Lebanon region in 1906. The couple made their way up the Hudson River, and since family were already here, they settled in Little Falls, New York. It is here that this typical Ellis Island immigrant story ends. For the next twenty-four years, Louis Mulkoon was in and out of trouble. It was of his own doing, and he would someday pay the ultimate price.

For several years, Mulkoon and his wife ran a small store on Flint Avenue. It was a modest establishment, like many corner stores in the city, but other stores could not compete with his prices. Most of the stock on his shelves were not wholesale-priced goods, but they *were* wholesale stolen goods. This came to light in April 1919, when Little Falls police apprehended two men burglarizing the West Shore Freight House. Brought to the Herkimer County Jail, the two felons were placed in separate cells and signed their confessions. Much to the surprise of Sheriff Leo Lawrence, each man in his confessions pointed the finger to Louis Mulkoon. They claimed that he had paid them in advance to break into the freight station. The stolen goods, they told Lawrence, were to be brought to Mulkoon's store for resale. Police immediately arrested Mulkoon.[25]

The fine Mulkoon paid was a minor setback in his business ventures. With the country coming to terms with Prohibition, Mulkoon saw his dream of fast money within his grasp. With stills scattered about the county, Mulkoon, with his son, Rocco, was only too happy to supply the thirsty residents of Little Falls with liquor. In fact, bootlegging was a Mulkoon family affair. On September 11, 1920, Sadie Mulkoon was arrested for selling "spirits and home brewed beer."[26]

By the 1920s, the Mulkoon family had worn out their welcome in Little Falls and moved on to bigger and what they thought were better things. For the next decade, they moved around the city of Utica in an attempt to make money selling alcohol and staying at least one step ahead of the law. This was difficult given their penchant for publicity. Many small-time bootleggers, for their own safety, avoided having their names in the press. This wasn't the case with Louis Mulkoon. In November 1927, Mulkoon reported to police that one evening, while he and his wife were out of the house, someone broke in and emptied his safe of $1,300. The thief, claimed Mulkoon, must have been someone who knew the combination to the safe, as "it was not even scratched." The Utica police, aware of the shady Mulkoon, simply brushed aside the incident. "Police Are Doubtful Anyone Took $1300" is how the *Utica Observer Dispatch* reported the latest Mulkoon story.[27]

Like his father, Rocco Mulkoon had his share of run-ins with the law. Actually, most of Rocco's troubles stemmed from running into cars in Utica. Listed as a "chauffer" in the 1930 Oneida County Census, Rocco was frequently involved in accidents racing about Utica in his truck. Why he was in such a hurry and what was he carrying in his truck was anyone's guess.

On September 25, 1930, Louis Mulkoon was poised to make the biggest move of his bootlegging career. Throughout the day, his wife, Sadie, recalled that her husband received three phone calls. Although she didn't eavesdrop, Sadie was quite certain that these phone calls had to do with her husband's bootlegging activities. These suspicions were confirmed when a small parade of men came to their 638 Elizabeth Street apartment. First to arrive on their doorstep was his upstairs neighbor. At the dinner table, Louis Mulkoon asked his neighbor if he could borrow $500.[28] With the country in the throes of the Great Depression, $500 was not pocket change. Mulkoon said he needed the money to invest in the purchase of a large still in Herkimer County.

A short while later, two more men arrived from Little Falls. Both were on the receiving end of alcohol supplied by Mulkoon and expressed interest in this latest business venture. Mulkoon assured everyone present that this was the deal of a lifetime. He was going to meet with a few men, "business partners," and they were going to buy $25,000 worth of "vats and materials" for only $500. The best part of the deal, he assured them, was that this deal came with police protection. Intrigued, all the men present wanted to know more about this "protection." A boastful Mulkoon said there was "going to be a new sheriff—a friend of mine who will do a thing for me."[29] The three men there should have thought long and hard about this statement. The "new" sheriff was Leo Lawrence, and he wasn't about to dole out favors to anyone, least of all a man with Mulkoon's reputation. Still, the men appeared to be satisfied, at least for the moment. All three of Mulkoon's guests went home when they were told that these new "business partners" were expected.

In the meantime, Rocco Mulkoon paced the floors incessantly, all the while reminding his father that they had to get ready to make the long drive to Frankfort. Louis tried to calm his impatient son, but it was no use. A knock

Crime scene photos. *From the Paul Draheim Collection at the Herkimer County Historical Society.*

on the apartment door broke the tension. The two men Louis Mulkoon had been expecting were on his doorstep. He turned, bid his wife goodbye and left the apartment. With his son by his side, Louis got behind the wheel of his automobile and followed the lead car driving toward Frankfort.

Around dusk, sixty-three-year-old Walter McGill, a Coop Hill farmer, was standing on his front porch when he heard what he believed to be the voices of men shouting somewhere in the vicinity of Jones Road. The shouting abruptly ended and was quickly followed by what McGill described as a "barrage of shots."[30] McGill got back into his house as fast as he could, locked the door and turned out all the lights. The only sound that broke the silence of the night was that of a car speeding past his house. The next day, McGill gingerly walked over to Jones Road and made a ghastly discovery. He returned home immediately and contacted the police.

When the police arrived at Jones Road, they were equally as horrified as McGill. One newspaper called it the epitome of "bootlegging vengeance."[31] Several feet from the automobile, near a barbed wire fence, lay the body of Louis Mulkoon. The coroner, Dr. James W. Graves, told the police that the elder Mulkoon didn't die instantly from the single gunshot wound to the abdomen. Since both hands of the deceased had grasped grass and dirt, Dr. Graves deduced that the man was writhing in pain as he slowly died. The autopsy concluded that Louis Mulkoon had died from a .45-caliber bullet and a single shotgun blast to the chest. On the opposite side of the road, near the automobile, was Rocco Mulkoon. According to the press, Rocco "had been shot several times through the body with a revolver while the top of his head and side of his face had been literally blown off by a shot gun."[32] In his pocket was a wallet containing $249 and on one hand was a diamond ring. The "business partners" who lured father and son to Jones Road were, in fact, their executioners.

The tiny leads the police had led nowhere. Friends, neighbors and even fellow bootleggers were interviewed and could not or would not assist in the investigation. Some said it was rival gang members from Albany who lured the two to Jones Road. Rumors persisted that the two were killed because their bootlegging operation was too successful. Louis Mulkoon, it was rumored, lowered his prices to drive out competitors in the area around Little Falls.

On October 30, 1930, Dr. Graves terminated the inquest into the deaths of Louis and Rocco Mulkoon, citing "a lack of evidence." A Herkimer grand jury followed suit. At least a half-dozen persons were brought in to testify at the courthouse, but as with the coroner's inquest, no real evidence could be produced. To this day, no one has been able to solve the murders.

In life, as in death, Louis and Rocco Mulkoon were inseparable. The father and son are buried together at Calvary Cemetery in Utica, New York.

A Wolf in Sheep's Clothing

By Donna Rubin

The neighbors might have seen it coming some years before, but the build-up over those decades was so long and so gradual that when it finally happened, they were shocked. Then again, with hindsight, who could really claim to be surprised?

John Henry House was born in 1857. His parents, Gaylord and Nancy Ann Skinner House, were both descended from early settlers in the area, and John Henry's childhood was spent on the family farm between Millers Mills and Columbia Center, which were busy hubs of commerce and social activity in those years. After finishing at the local one-room school, he took a course at Utica Business College, from which he graduated in 1882.

Returning to the family farm, he soon married Cora Thankful Firman in 1883. She was a graduate of the Winfield Academy, a teacher and an accomplished musician. His parents had moved to another house on the property, and the newlyweds took over the home farm, where their four children arrived over the next eight years. Shortly following the birth of their last child, Cora took the children and returned to her parents' home to live. Apparently, domestic bliss was not to be found at Highview Sheep Farm. Two years later, in 1893, Cora allowed John Henry to divorce her, with the condition that she retain custody of the children.

By this time, John Henry had become a well-regarded and successful sheep farmer and was active in the Millers Mills community. Over the years, he was Sunday school superintendent of the local Baptist church, a charter member of the new Millers Mills Grange, an officer in the cemetery association and the local telephone company, a member of the Board of Assessors and the Board of Elections and a district school clerk. He married his second wife, Mary Eva Hadcox of Richfield, in 1894, when he was thirty-seven. Sadly, Eva and her baby died shortly after birth the next year.

The lonely widower must have found it difficult to convince any of the local ladies to join him at his farm on the hills, for he turned to the Utica newspapers and advertised for a housekeeper. Arriving at the little Millers Mills depot by train, Mrs. Clara Maria Kasson Davis Little settled in at the isolated farmhouse and, barely more than year after Eva's death, became the third Mrs. House.

Left: Cora Firman. *Right*: Mrs. Harriet House.

Life on the farm wasn't the idyllic country retreat Clara had expected. She was accustomed to exhausting physical work, but living with John Henry's controlling, jealous nature turned out to be a challenge. She began visiting neighboring farm wives Mrs. Getman and Mrs. Wiskins, complaining of his "brutal and bestial" behavior and showing evidence of his abuse. She consulted Dr. Cristman of Columbia Center for treatment and advice and was prescribed "quieting medicine." She acquired a revolver for her protection and at one time even packed to leave the farm, but she stayed because she feared John Henry's reprisal. Finally, one day in the spring of 1900, she told Mrs. Wiskins that if anything should happen to her, she should get in touch with her sister.

Something did happen to her on the evening of May 10 that year. Returning to the house after doing chores, John Henry found his wife dead on the parlor floor, with a rope around her neck. A six-inch iron hook had been pulled out of the wall, and a kitchen chair was overturned. John Henry sent a telegram to Clara's sister in New Hampshire, and she and her husband came to Herkimer to take the body home for burial. But tipped off by suspicious neighbors, the Herkimer County district attorney intercepted the little group at the train station and had the casket unloaded from the train and taken away, pending an investigation. Although there was testimony about John Henry's abusiveness from Cora, the first Mrs. House, there was insufficient evidence to bring charges. Clara's death was ruled a suicide.

The intimidating physical appearance of John Henry had been noted by the newspapers when he attended the inquest at Herkimer: "tall, massive in build, standing 6 feet, stalwart, bronzed, a man of mammoth stature, and powerful." This is what greeted Adelaide Allen in 1901, when she arrived at the Millers Mills station, responding to an ad for a "housekeeper." The couple married within months, but Addie herself was experienced in the "practice" of matrimony, previously having been married three or four times herself. In less than a year, Mrs. House no. 4 fled the farm and filed for a decree of separation, alleging cruel and inhuman treatment. For the next five years, John Henry was ordered to make support payments, until the divorce was finalized in 1907.

For more than fifteen years, John Henry continued to advertise and "housekeepers" continued to respond, but none stayed for very long until Mrs. Harriet Lawrence Cook Schmall arrived in 1923. She, too, brought her own interesting marital history with her. Within months of marrying John Henry, she left the Millers Mills farm on May 5, 1924, taking a housekeeping job at the Jacob Shaul home at nearby Columbia Center. She began separation proceedings immediately, giving testimony of abuse, and a final separation settlement, awarding her twenty dollars' monthly support, was scheduled for June 28. She planned to leave immediately for Watertown after the hearing, where she would live with her son's family.

John Henry House.

On Thursday evening, June 26, at about seven o'clock, Jake Shaul returned to the house after barn chores. Expecting to find supper on the table, what he found instead took away any thought of food. Lying on the kitchen floor, in a pool of congealing blood, was the body of his housekeeper, Harriet House, obviously dead. An autopsy would detail the fatal wounds: the head nearly severed, a five-inch slit across the throat gaping one and a half inches, a three-and-a-half-inch slit on the back of the neck gaping two inches and a stab wound penetrating the liver. Mr. Shaul called Dr. Merton Brown, and the doctor contacted the coroner, Dr. Manion. Deputy Sheriff Ralph Cress and Assistant District Attorney James Greene hurried to the grisly scene. After making arrangements with photographer Fred Abbott to take pictures of the crime area, they collected a few local young men who were especially strong and drove two miles to the House farm. When confronted with the facts, John Henry readily admitted to killing Harriet, telling authorities that he had acted in self-defense. He was handcuffed and taken to the Herkimer jail. It was now close to midnight.

It turned out that John Henry had shown up at the Shaul place late in the afternoon on Thursday under the pretext of collecting some tools that he accused Harriet of taking from the farm. According to John Henry, they argued about the tools. Harriet picked up a butcher knife to attack him, and he grabbed the knife and turned it on her. He then wiped it on her clothes, dropped it and left, "while she was still kicking." He said he went back to the farm and did evening chores as usual and then listened on the phone while neighbors talked about the gory event at "the Center." He wasn't surprised when authorities showed up to escort him to Herkimer.

Those investigating determined another scenario. Finding an empty case for a straight razor on the floor at the scene and no sign of a butcher knife, it was decided that a razor had been the weapon; the crime was thus premeditated, as the razor would have been brought there for no other reason.

John Henry remained in the Herkimer County Jail, awaiting a grand jury that wouldn't meet until November. As he waited through the summer days, he was examined by two state alienists, who determined he was sane and fit to stand trial. Meanwhile, the crime scene at Columbia Center and the House farm near Millers Mills were visited by hundreds of curious visitors, who paid Jake Shaul ten cents to see what they had only read about.

But by July 10, John Henry was tired of waiting, and after writing a letter to a cousin giving his version of the events, he threw a towel over a gas pipe in his cell and hanged himself, thus relieving Herkimer County and the State of New York of the expense of months of confinement, a trial and, undoubtedly, an execution.

WAGNER-HOTALING MURDER OF LITTLE FALLS

By Susan Perkins

Thomas Wagner of Little Falls, New York, was born in 1904, the son of August and Carrie Wagner. Golda Hotaling was born in 1908, the daughter of Laverne and Elizabeth Hotaling. Wagner first met Golda when the Hotalings were living on Burwell Street. They resumed their acquaintance when he started to visit a friend at the Hotaling residence on Summit Avenue, where he eventually became a boarder. Thomas and Golda became romantically involved and were married on January 16, 1925, in Little Falls, unbeknownst to her family. They sent a telegram from Syracuse notifying her parents of the nuptials.

They continued to live with Golda's parents and her eight siblings. Thomas was a spinner at one of the knitting mills, and Golda was a packer at the hammer factory. They were able to get an apartment together in a rooming house at 337 South Ann Street, but by August of the next year, marital troubles had ensued; the couple separated, with Golda returning to live with her parents and Thomas renting a room in the upper part of the same house. Thomas made appeals to her to come back and live with him, but she refused.

The couple finally went to see Little Falls attorney Edmund McCarthy to discuss separation papers. But Thomas changed his mind and visited his wife at the Cheney hammer plant where she was employed, telling her that he was not going to apply for separation.

On August 31, 1926, Thomas met Golda on the street and asked to speak to her. He was seen taking her by the arm, and he brought her back to the rooming house on Ann Street. The landlady, Mrs. Jones, was happy to see the couple together again and gave them the use of the living room, closing the door to give them privacy. Off the living room was a bedroom, where an argument quickly ensued. Golda told her husband, "If you don't keep away from me I'll kill you," and Thomas retorted back that he would kill her. She started for the door, and he grabbed her by the throat. She called out, "Mrs. Jones!" but no one heard her cry. Thomas continued to choke her until she fell backward on the bed and he fell on top of her. He later stated that she was unconscious when he left to head immediately to police headquarters, where he reported what had happened.

When Police Chief Long, accompanied by Officer Francis Reardon, arrived at the scene, they discovered the body of Mrs. Wagner laying across

GOLDA HOTALING WAGNER

the bed lifeless. Thomas was remanded to the Herkimer County Jail, where he was the lone prisoner on the third floor, in Chester Gillette's old cell. He spent his time reading many of the newspapers that gave accounts of his crime. He asked for no other reading material. He told Sheriff Goodrich that he was comfortable and his surroundings satisfactory. On September 4, 1926, his only visitors were his brother, Raymond, and his counsel, attorney James P. O'Donnell.

His trial commenced on December 27. Local newspapers reported on his "coolness" of character while he was in jail and at the trial. District Attorney Greene outlined the charges made by the prosecution, followed by the defense, which stated that it would prove that Golda Wagner's death was not caused by asphyxiation but rather by apoplexy and that it was not premeditated, asking for a sentence of second-degree manslaughter.

The testimony of medical witnesses would disprove the defense's first contention. The four doctors testifying all claimed that death was caused by "asphyxiation due to strangulation," giving graphic details on what happens to a person when strangled. Other witnesses included Golda's sister, Mildred Hotaling, who testified that the couple never quarreled when they lived with her parents. When Golda returned home, he tried to visit her there, and one evening, Golda had told him she had a "date." The date was with her sister, Mildred. While the sister was giving her testimony, it was noted that Thomas sat there smiling.

When it was his turn on the stand, Thomas admitted to choking his wife to stop her from crying out. He was angry because "she would not wait and listen until I talked our troubles over." After he realized what he had done, he ran from the house frightened and went directly to the police station.

Attorney O'Donnell made a plea for leniency, "asking the court to take into consideration 'the frailties of human nature,'" noting, "It was evident that Wagner was not born with a calm and even temper."

According to the *Evening Times* on December 31, "His face, serious as the jury filed into the court room, lighted with a smile when the foreman, C.J. Falk announced 'we find the defendant guilty of manslaughter, first degree.' Wagner started up from his chair and clapped his hands together. He was tapped on the shoulder by a deputy, who told him not to be so expressive." He had escaped a murder conviction. Judge Bell sentenced him "to Auburn Prison for not less than 10 nor more than 20 years."

On January 12, 1927, Wagner was taken from Herkimer to begin his prison term. In the 1930 census, Wagner was identified as an inmate at Auburn State Prison. His occupation was listed as prison hospital attendant.

After he got out of jail, Thomas used his experience at that hospital to become a surgical technician in the army, enlisting on October 20, 1942, to serve his country overseas in World War II. At that time, he also remarried, to nurse Catherine Carroll, and they lived at 923 Adams Street in Syracuse. After the war, he continued his military career in the Army Medical Department, but his marriage did not last. His wife, Catherine, remarried to a Charles Fisher in 1947. Thomas stayed in the service for more than twenty years, attaining the rank of master sergeant and retiring on October 31, 1962. In an obituary for his niece Eleanor Kukowski in 1981 in the *Utica Daily Press*, he is listed as a surviving family member as "Mr. and Mrs. Thomas Wagner of San Antonio, Texas," so he did remarry again. Thomas died on June 10, 1983, in Universal City, Texas. We could not find an obituary for him.

Golda is buried at the Rural Park Cemetery in Inghams Mills.

THE FINAL ARGUMENT

By Ted Adams

Coming back to Herkimer to the residence of his wife, Lottie, apparently to do away with her, proved fatal to Frank Novakowski on May 2, 1927. He had been living in Rochester, estranged from his wife for two and a half years. He came back to Herkimer fully armed. There is no question that murder was on his mind. He arrived in Herkimer on a Wednesday and made threats to his wife, who was living with her parents, Mr. and Mrs. Enoch Golicki, at 331 South Washington Street. He was unhappy about paying his wife child support for their two children, Edmund and Frank, ages eight and five.

Above: Theo home of Mr. and Mrs. Enoch Golicki.

Left: Officer Joseph Butts.

Opposite: Neighborhood kids crowd in to get a glimpse as the body of Frank Novak is brought out.

Frank Novakowski used the alias Frank Novak. Mrs. Novakowski stated that Frank returned to the house late Sunday night under the influence of liquor. He went to the room where his wife was sleeping, pointed a revolver and told her to go downstairs. She made an excuse that she had to get her shoes and awakened her father. The father and Frank had a tussle. Lottie ran to the street to call for help, and Frank broke free and fired two shots at her. She fell to the street. Thinking he hit her, he turned and fired three shots through the window at his father-in-law and fled. All shots missed. Word got to the police station, and patrolman Joe Butts responded and stayed the night at the residence. He was relieved by another officer but returned around ten o'clock. Frank showed up again, threatening Officer Butts and firing two shots at him but missing both. Butts drew his gun and fired three times. All three hit Frank, and he died as a result.

This proved quite a lot of excitement in the neighborhood, and this incident of gunplay in Herkimer resonated throughout the valley.

Lottie Novak went on to marry Raymond Kozlowski on October 20, 1930, and they operated several tavern and restaurant establishments in the Middleville and Newport area, including Lottie's Tavern and the Lake House in Middleville and the Black Dahlia, located on Route 28 between Newport and Poland. The Black Dahlia was destroyed by fire in 1964. I recall the place and was there a few times, but it was a bit expensive for me as a young person. As I remember, many people from Utica made the trip to Poland for good food and entertainment.

The photographs here, including the one of Novak's body being taken out of the home where the incident took place, were found in the collection of Herkimer County historian Paul Draheim. A newspaper report from the *Herkimer Telegram-Record*, dated May 3, 1927, noted, "Nathan Kurland took photographs of the South Washington street residence and at the undertaking parlors." We are not sure if these photos were taken by Draheim or if Kurland had taken them and Draheim somehow obtained the pictures. They are now in the collection of the Herkimer County Historical Society.

THE TRESPASSING COWS

By Margaret Sinclair

As you will soon see, the author is telling this story from the perspective of the accused murderer, with the scenario that he is in prison at the end of his life reflecting on what has taken place.

It's November 1945. I am seventy-five years old and feeling like the end is coming. I'm sitting in my cell at Dannemora prison reflecting on my life. I came here from Auburn Correctional. I hadn't planned for my life to turn out this way.

Forgive me for not introducing myself. I am Michael Camerano, aka Carlo Francesco. I was born in Padula, Italy, in 1870. My childhood was pretty uneventful until I was suspected of conspiring to kill my uncle. I didn't know what to do, so I sailed to America. I was tried *in absentia*, found guilty and sentenced to twenty-three years in prison. (In Italy, the sentence starts immediately, whether you are there or not.) My wife, Margaret, and I started a new life in America. We settled in a small upstate community known as Frankfort. I had a farm on what is known as "the reservation" where we raised our sons and daughter. Life was good.

On October 22, 1926, I went to my farm to work and found that my neighbor David Reese's cows were trampling through my orchard. His fence had a hole in it. I went to see Mr. Reese, as I'd never had a problem with him, and told him what was happening. He agreed to pay for my damages and ordered his hired man, LeRoy Sweet, to fix the fence. The next day, the cattle were back in my orchard, and I again complained to Mr. Reese. Mr. Sweet called me names and wanted to fight me. I went to the local authorities and pleaded my case. They refused to issue a warrant.

The next day, I was showing a customer where to pick apples in my orchard, and Sweet was spreading manure in the next field. He threw a rock at me and told me he'd like to put a fork in me. I grabbed my shotgun, which I often took to the farm with me in case a rabbit appeared. I waited in the brush and shot at Sweet as he passed by in his wagon. He kept going, so I figured I missed. I later learned he had died from shotgun wounds. Before he passed away, he told authorities that I shot him.

I didn't know what to do, so I hid in the woods for a day and then made my way to New York City by walking and hitching rides when I could. I stayed with Peter and Christine Lambiaso, friends of mine on Long Island. I shaved

Returning on the boat from Italy. Sheriff J.C. Rasbach and Deputy Sheriff Adam M. Allen traveled to Italy to bring Camerano (*center*) back to the United States. The two men with him are not identified.

From left to right: District Attorney Carl W. Peterson, Sheriff Leo Lawrence, Michael Camerano and turnkey Charles Daniels at the Herkimer County Jail.

my moustache, changed my name and got a job as a night watchman. I later learned that the Lambiasos' were charged with aiding a fugitive. They told authorities they didn't know I was a fugitive. Christine was shown mercy, as she was pregnant with her tenth child. Peter did not fare as well. He was sent to prison for between fourteen and eighteen months.

On July 4, a local policeman started asking me questions. It made me fearful, so I left for Boston. I was working there for about two years when I got word that my mother was not doing well. So, on December 28, 1928, I sailed for my hometown of Padula, Italy. It was there that I met and married Antoinette. (I never received any letters from my first wife, so I guess she moved on.) Antoinette and I had a little girl. My wife and daughter were very important to me, and I still have their picture. She was only nine months old when they took me away. She must be a beautiful young lady by now. Things in Padula were good until my brother, Antone, and I quarreled over a piece of property that my mother had left. He turned me in to authorities. I was put in jail and worked as a shoemaker in prison. My beautiful young wife and baby girl visited me weekly. I was there about nine months when a detective from New York City, Michael Bernibec, got wind of me. He happened to be in Italy on other business. He had been looking for me for the murder of Sweet. Apparently, there was quite a reward on my head, so it didn't take long for Bernibec to notify authorities in Herkimer County.

Governor Roosevelt appealed to Mussolini to extradite me. Do you know that I became the first Italian to be extradited? Sheriff J.C. Rasbach sailed to Italy to arrest me and take me back to America. We set sail on November 25, 1930, on the ship *Saturnia*. Of course, my time was spent in the brig. Sheriff Rasbach brought me back to Herkimer County under guard and in secret.

I was not happy to be in the Herkimer County Jail. They placed me in Chester Gillette's cell. That is where all those accused of murder are held. I remained despondent even after my wife and grandson visited me. She knew the jail was drafty and brought me warm clothes. I was facing the electric chair. Did people expect me to be joyous? Leo Lawrence took over as sheriff, and he advised me that I could plead to second-degree manslaughter to avoid execution. I felt much better then, and my disposition improved. Attorney Chester J. Winslow from Frankfort was appointed to represent me. He agreed that I would change my plea. I was sentenced to twenty years to life at Auburn State Prison. I thanked the court for its leniency. Sheriff Lawrence transported me to the Correctional Facility, where I began my sentence.

I never meant to hurt anyone. It was those damn trespassing cows.

Michael Camerano died at Dannemora on December 1, 1945.

THE BREWER MYSTERY

By James Greiner

A reporter for the *Utica Daily Press* echoed what a great many people had said all along: Leo Lawrence was "a man of keen personality and one of the county's most popular residents, [who] has worked from the 'bottom' so to speak."[33]

Born on April 26, 1896, in Mohawk, New York, there was very little in the childhood background of Leo Lawrence to suggest that he would become one of the most successful civil servants in the history of Herkimer County. The reason for this is that he simply didn't have an ordinary childhood.

A defining moment in the life of Leo Lawrence occurred on November 27, 1911, when his father was attempting to cross between two freight cars that were stalled at the railroad crossing on North Prospect Street. His father was halfway over the car coupler when the train suddenly jolted. Losing his balance and his grip, the elder Lawrence tumbled beneath the rolling cars. Unable to scramble to safety in time, his left foot became wedged under a wheel and was slowly crushed. There was little the doctors at Little Falls Hospital could do but amputate his foot at the ankle.[34]

With the family beset by hospital bills, not to mention a father who could not work, the fourteen-year-old Lawrence made an adult decision. He quit school and tended the family grocery store at the corner of Bellinger Avenue and Bellinger Street. He devoted whatever spare time he had to schoolwork with the hopes of completing his education. Three years later, Leo Lawrence returned to Herkimer High School and amazed everyone. He graduated with the class of 1915 and at the graduation ceremony was awarded "$5 in gold, being the student making the most commendable effort to obtain an education."[35] His next stop was Georgetown University.

When America entered the First World War, Lawrence set Georgetown aside and enlisted as a naval air cadet. Although he was never posted overseas, he managed to earn his wings and become a flight instructor for the giant NC-4 float plane. When the war was over, he returned home to Herkimer and reacquainted himself with his father's expanding grocery business. As the years went by, Leo Lawrence was spending less time in the store and more time delving into local politics. In the spring of 1930, he announced his intentions to run for the office of Herkimer County sheriff. He canvassed the county seeking votes and in September won the Republican primary, fending off eight challengers. Two months later, in the county-wide election, ten candidates appeared on the ballot. When it was announced that Lawrence had been victorious, the *Utica Daily Press* lauded the ambitions of the thirty-year-old as "believed to be one of the nation's youngest sheriffs."[36]

On January 1, 1931, newly sworn in sheriff Leo Lawrence and his wife, Verna, ascended the limestone staircase of the county jail. The front portion of the jail would be their new residence for the next three years. They hadn't unpacked many of their belongings when he received a phone call. A snow-covered body had been discovered near the New York Central Railroad tracks west of Frankfort. It was his first day on the job, and the man with no official police training had a dead body to deal with. Fortunately for Leo Lawrence, a man who did have a lot of experience in this line of work, Dr. James W. Graves, was there to assist him.

By the time Graves and Lawrence arrived in the area of west Frankfort, a small crowd had gathered. A reporter from the *Utica Daily Press* was already

Sheriff Leo Lawrence. After being sheriff of Herkimer County, he became a New York State assemblyman from 1936 to 1964.

Crime scene photo. *From the Paul Draheim Collection at the Herkimer County Historical Society.*

taking notes for his story, while photographer H. Paul Draheim leveled his camera at the body that lay between the east- and westbound tracks. Several people from the neighboring houses looked about curiously, wondering what had happened. While Dr. Graves walked down the small embankment to the tracks, Lawrence sought out the person who had discovered the body.

Edward T. Ferguson stepped forward and said that he was in Tower 29 when he received word from a westbound freight train at 1:52 p.m. He was informed that there was something, perhaps a body, near the tracks. Ferguson went on to say that he left his post and went out to the location immediately. Ferguson pointed to the road where Lawrence had parked his car. He told the sheriff that he went up to the road and hailed a passing car. The motorist was Raymond C. Staley. It was he who alerted the authorities.[37]

Meanwhile, Dr. Graves was doing a preliminary examination of the corpse. When told by Sheriff Lawrence that Staley had called authorities between 2:10 p.m. and 2:25 p.m., Dr. Graves's suspicions were confirmed. "The man had been dead but a short time before I arrived." While deputies attended to the body, Dr. Graves stepped forward and issued a small statement to the press: "Frederick B. Brewer came to his death in an accidental manner, unknown at this time. It is possible that he may have been passenger on an eastbound train that left Utica between 19 and 11 A.M. yesterday. The investigation will be continued to determine if possible, the details."[38] When Graves released the name of the deceased, the press as well as the police went to work.

Working closely with the Utica police, Leo Lawrence learned that the dead man between the tracks was Frederick B. Brewer of 117 Clinton Place, Utica. He was a 1916 graduate of Colgate University, where he was the manager of the football team. Brewer served aboard a submarine in the war, was president of the Utica Alumni Chapter of Colgate University and was a member of the Utica Elks. He was thirty-five years old, resided with his widowed mother and was currently employed as a securities bond salesman with the National City Company of New York. News of his death reverberated about the city of Utica. Under the front-page headline "Mystery Attends Utican's Death," the *Utica Daily Press* reported that Brewer "was [a] well known salesman and well known in financial and social circle." That day, the press as well as the police received hundreds of telephone calls and noted that Brewer's mother "bore up well with the news of her son's death."[39] Phone calls from the general public, however, yielded few clues to assist the police in solving this mystery. From all appearances, Fred Brewer was a well-liked individual with no enemies.

His mother and his close friends could offer no plausible explanation as to what had happened.

The supposition proposed by Dr. Graves that Brewer had fallen from a train was dashed when the police went to Union Station in Utica. The ticket master remembered Brewer. He recalled that Brewer was there with a woman and purchased only one ticket. When the police asked if he was certain, the ticket master replied that there could be no mistake. The train was running thirty minutes late that day, and Brewer and the lady sat across the office and visited. When the train arrived, Brewer escorted the lady to the train car and then left the station alone. It was later learned that the lady he took to the station was, in fact, his cousin Leta Bentley.[40]

But how did Frederick Brewer get to the railroad tracks in Frankfort? On January 5, William Baxter, a driver for the Black and White Taxi Company, came forward. "I am not accustomed to picking up strangers," said Baxter, who was off duty at the time, "but this chap looked like a nice young man and it was slippery walking so I asked him if he wanted a ride. He got in and rode with me until I turned off the main road, which is quite near the railroad."

Baxter gave a fairly accurate description of the mysterious stranger to the police. His height, hair color, complexion and overcoat were a perfect match to that of Brewer. "I noted that his coat wasn't buttoned and that he had no mittens, I remember that because I spoke about it and he said he wasn't cold." Sheriff Lawrence as well as Dr. Graves noted that the deceased wasn't wearing a hat when they inspected the body. The gray felt hat described by Baxter was located quite a distance away, blown past the body, do doubt, by the draft from a passing train. The hat only added to the mystery. When the police presented it to Baxter's mother, she claimed to have never seen it. Her son, she informed the authorities, always wore a bowler hat.[41] Later, Lawrence discovered that the man who had discovered the body, Edward T. Fergusson, confessed to dragging the body away from the tracks. His explanation was that he didn't want the body near the passing trains. Lawrence shook his head in disbelief. Now it was impossible to determine the exact location of the body, and if there was any other evidence, it was either washed away due to the weather or blown from the tracks by passing trains.

Things didn't look any better when Dr. Graves released his coroner's report. Frederick Brewer, said Graves, died "due to shock from a fracture at the base of the skull and hemorrhage from a puncture of the left lung, which he received in an unknown manner."[42] Now the police were beginning to second-guess themselves. A punctured lung together with a blunt-force trauma wound to the lower skull didn't have the hallmarks of a suicide or an accident. Perhaps Frederick Brewer was murdered.

Frederick Brewer was buried on January 3, 1931, at Forest Hill Cemetery in Utica. Several days later, on January 6, the *Utica Daily Press* underscored the frustration experienced by Herkimer and Oneida police agencies under the headline "Brewer Mystery Still Unsolved."[43] At every turn, there appeared to be another unanswered question. When it was learned that Brewer had given up his postal box several days before his death, relatives came forward and said that he had left his job as a salesman with the National City Company of New York and no longer required the box. Granted, selling bonds during the first years of the Great Depression was difficult, but that doesn't really answer the questions as to why he quit this job. Added to this, it was learned that Brewer let his $10,000 life insurance policy lapse on December 31, the day before he died.[44]

Herkimer County district attorney Carl Peterson announced that his office would not comment or commit itself to any course of action concerning Brewer's death until Sheriff Lawrence produced some sort of evidence. At the same time, Dr. Graves wouldn't convene a coroner's inquest, as no witnesses had stepped forward. In Utica, the police suspended their investigation until new evidence came to light. To this day, no one has been able to explain what really happened to Frederick Brewer.

TAKEN FOR A RIDE: PAOLO BASILE

By James Greiner

The same day the bullet-riddled corpses of Louis and Rocco Mulkoon were discovered in Frankfort, Utica detectives paid a visit to the Castle Restaurant on 801 Bleecker Street. With speakeasies scattered throughout east Utica, the detectives had good reason to choose this particular establishment. The proprietor of the establishment, "known as a maker and seller of cheap liquor," not only knew Louis Mulkoon but also worked for him. His name was Paolo Basile.[45]

Leaving his wife and child in Italy, Paolo Basile came to America in 1919 to make money. He was a tinsmith by trade and a still maker by choice. By the late 1920s, Basile's services were in demand. He was regarded as one of the premier still makers in the Mohawk Valley. When detectives told him what had transpired on Jones Road in Frankfort, Basile was unmoved and stoically expressed little concern. He led police to believe that this sort of thing was to be expected. According to Basile, Louis and Rocco Mulkoon talked too much for their own good. In his opinion, both of them were nothing more than "squealers." They asked too many questions about the whereabouts of stills between Utica and Frankfort. Word on the street, said Basile, was that father and son were trying to get rid of the competition by tipping off federal agents as to the location of these stills. This air of indifference on the part of Basile didn't fool the detectives. They knew all about him and his business partnership with the Mulkoons. If the ill-fated Mulkoons had an enemy, Basile would know who it was, and right now he wasn't about to squeal.[46]

Paolo Basile resided with his nephew Dominick Cognetti at 1200 Blandina Street. Late in the afternoon of November 27, 1930, Basile received a phone call and abruptly left his nephew's house. This immediately aroused the suspicions of Cognetti. His uncle was always in the habit of telling him where he was going, who he was meeting and what time to expect him home. Basile took his 1930 Ford coupe and drove to the Venezia Coffee House on Bleecker Street. Here he drank and played cards with friends while awaiting for a phone call. At 9:00 p.m., Basile received his call. "Well boys," he said, "I must leave to attend to some business. See you all later."[47]

When Basile failed to return home, his nephew became worried. Making his way down Bleecker Street, Cognetti went to his uncle's favorite spots and made inquiries. It was at Venezia's that he learned of the mysterious phone call his uncle received. Basile's card-playing friends told Cognetti that his uncle was headed down Bleecker Street. Getting into his car, Cognetti drove off, hoping to catch a glimpse of the Ford coupe. Was there a chance his uncle had gone to some other speakeasy? As it turned out, this was wishful thinking. Cognetti found his uncle's car at the corner of Elizabeth and Hubbell Streets. The driver-side door was wide open, and the keys were still in the ignition. Cognetti went immediately to the police station.[48]

Not surprisingly, the police investigation into the disappearance of Paolo Basile yielded only rumors. Some claimed that fearing for his life, he had gone into hiding in Chicago. Some believed he had gone to Buffalo to stay with other members of the Basile family. When it was discovered that he had emptied his checking account at the Utica branch of the Citizen's Trust Company the day before he disappeared, some surmised that he had gone back to Italy.[49] When a canceled check was returned dated November 28, the day after he disappeared, police tracked down the recipient, only to be disappointed. The insurance agent to whom the check was made out told the police that Basile, for some unknown reason, backdated the check.[50]

As weeks passed, the police learned that Basile may have been experiencing financial problems. At the time of his disappearance, a local grocery store was ready to start a civil action against him and the Mulkoon estate for an unpaid bill of $1,000 for sugar. It was also whispered that Basile had been paid $1,000 in advance to build a still. Perhaps he took the money, gambled it away and ultimately paid with his life.[51]

As the public clamored for answers, Captain Stephen McGrath of the New York State Police urged everyone to be patient. "Everything possible will be done to solve this case," he said. "I understand that in and around Utica, it has been only a question of where the body would be found."[52] McGrath was right; it was only a question of time.

On April 14, 1931, Michael Powell was walking along the banks of the Barge Canal outside Frankfort. He was on his way to Ilion in hopes of finding a job when he suddenly noticed something peculiar in the canal. Powell couldn't quite make out what it was. He continued to stare at the buoyant mass, for that was all he could see, when a barge canal tugboat drew near. The ripple waves from the boat pushed the object closer to shore. The two men in the boat could see that it was a body and eventually so could Powell.[53]

Crime scene photo. *From the Paul Draheim Collection at the Herkimer County Historical Society.*

Crime scene photo. *From the Paul Draheim Collection at the Herkimer County Historical Society.*

By the time law enforcement officials arrived, the body had been dragged ashore. Herkimer County coroner Dr. James W. Graves was the first to approach the body and proceeded to give it a cursory examination. The head exhibited a large, deep wound, and the facial features were decomposed, almost unrecognizable, from being submerged in the water. Dr. Graves checked the pockets of the deceased. In one pocket was $12.15 and in the other a wallet. He opened the wallet, looked at the driver's license and then passed it off to a state policeman. It belonged to Paolo Basile.[54]

The discovery of Basile's body only intensified speculation as to who was responsible for the murder. Dr. Graves was thoroughly disappointed that his autopsy of Louis and Rocco Mulkoon produced little in the form of clues to assist the police in their investigation of that double homicide. He could only hope that this autopsy could help the police solve the murders of all three. Dr. Graves agreed with the Utica newspapers that the Mulkoon murders and the murder of Paolo Basile were connected.

In his report, Dr. Graves concluded that Paolo Basile did not drown. He was dead long before he went to his watery grave. He was strangled to death. The meat cleaver–sized wound to the head was just for good measure. What interested Graves was the sash cord garrote around Basile's neck. Finally, thought Dr. Graves, the police had a clue. One month earlier, on the night of February 8, the body of Philip DeSalvo was discovered at the eastern entrance of Proctor Park. He, too, was strangled to death with a sash cord.

It was the opinion of Dr. Graves and almost everyone else involved in the investigation that Basile was "taken for a ride." Some said that he "knew too much"—in fact, he probably knew the wrong people. The unsolved murder of Paolo Basile was the last time Depression-era gangs of Utica dumped their dirty laundry in Herkimer County.

THE LAST STILL RAID

By James Greiner

Before being led off to Utica to be officially charged with breaking several laws, H. Paul Draheim of the *Utica Observer Dispatch* made this photographic record of "The Last Still Raid."

Two of the most creative groups in the world are kids and criminals. Youngsters can make a go-kart out of junk in the garage or fashion a wallet out of an old baseball mitt. They simply have a lot of time on their hands, and they are always thinking. Criminals have a lot of time on their hands, too, but they think differently.

During the era of Prohibition, there were no more clever, ingenious people than bootleggers. These small-time entrepreneurs saw in America during this era a product and a profit. All you had to do was make or supply booze to a very thirsty public, collect your money and depend on gangsters as your sales representatives and for protection. Easy, right?

When Prohibition came to an end on December 5, 1933, it didn't necessarily mean that the bootleggers stood in bread lines with the rest of unemployed Americans during the Great Depression. On the contrary, business for bootleggers was just as good, if not better. Now that Prohibition had effectively come to an end, the government reinstituted the excise tax on alcohol. The alcohol produced by bootleggers in illegal stills all over the state was tax free. Between 1934 and 1938, the federal government estimated that it lost almost a total of $5 million in tax revenue from the more than twenty stills that were raided in Oneida County and three in Herkimer County.[55]

Conducting a raid on a still was a win-or-lose situation. The big win came when you raided an operational still, confiscated gallons of untaxed alcohol and made multiple arrests. You didn't always win. In April 1935, agents from the Alcohol Tax Unit (ATU), headquartered in Syracuse, led a

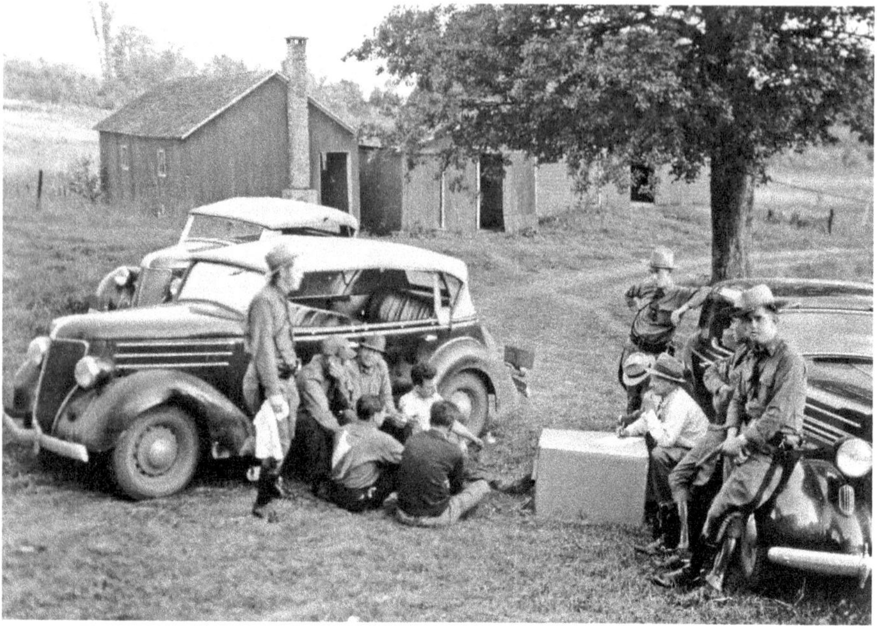

Crime scene photo. *From the Paul Draheim Collection at the Herkimer County Historical Society.*

raid on a still on Hiawatha Boulevard and literally came up empty-handed. The 750-gallon still, capable of producing 350 gallons of alcohol per day, was completely dry, as were the dozens of transport cans strewn about the warehouse. Not a single arrest was made.[56] ATU agents had to work as secretly as their adversaries if they wanted to succeed.

Agent Howard Edwards of the Utica ATU office was leaving nothing to chance when he learned of a still in Herkimer County. His preliminary investigation had already revealed that the old Jones farmhouse, situated between Russia Corners and Prospect, had been purchased in cash. Utica realtor John T. Kinney told Edwards that his wife had made the property transfer to a man named Ralph Lassandro. Agent Edwards wasn't surprised to learn that no such person existed.[57]

Using the same techniques he used on an August 8 still raid in the town of Schuyler, Edwards placed an agent nearby to monitor the activity in the vicinity of the old Jones farm. Cars came and went like clockwork. When one group of men showed up, another other group left. His lookout informed him that there were two shifts of three men each working a twelve-hour shift. After two weeks of surveillance, Edwards made preparations to raid the farmhouse. Leading the August 25 raid was Sergeant Joseph A. Seeley and Howard Ellsworth from the East Herkimer Station. They were joined by P.J. Corbett and William Keeley of the New Hartford Station.

The state police, together with several federal agents, arrived at the farmhouse at 6:15 a.m. Using their cars to block the roads leading away from the farmhouse, the troopers crept slowly toward the barn. Once behind the barn, Sergeant Joseph Seeley instructed his men to fan out and surround the farmhouse. At his signal, they would all rush the building. Pausing for a moment, Seeley watched as each man slowly made his way from behind the barn. Since he had the shortest distance to walk, Seeley wanted to give each man a chance to get into position. Slowly, Seeley emerged from behind the barn and quietly made his way to the front door of the farmhouse. He had only gone a few steps when the silence of the morning was shattered by the barking of a German Shepherd.

The watchdog at the front door of the house charged toward Seeley. The state policeman drew his service revolver and shot once, slightly grazing the dog. The wounded dog crawled into the farmhouse, with Seeley not far behind. Once inside, the dog lunged at him one last time. Seeley shot again and did not miss.[58]

A still raid roundup ends with smiles for the camera. *From the Paul Draheim Collection at the Herkimer County Historical Society.*

The sounds of the barking dog, along with the gunshots, ruined the element of surprise the police wanted, and pandemonium took over. The six bootleggers ran from the house as fast as they could in every direction. One by one they were chased down by the police and ATU agents. Soon, it became obvious to the authorities that this particular group of felons were amateurs. They never learned the number one rule when questioned by the police: always stick to the same story.

Elmer Pfanz tried to escape by jumping into the front seat of a car. He professed no knowledge of a still. "I was picking berries," he said. Joseph Sarcone was eventually found cowering in a field for a half hour. Covered with burdock, he told the police that he didn't know there was a still in the house. "I was picking berries." And finally there was Frank Tretto. "I was picking mushrooms." What, no berries? Frank Bumbolo, Natale Ormarso and Joseph Salemo agreed on their alibis. Still? What still?[59]

Federal agents said that the still in the old Jones farmhouse was about as elaborate a still they had come upon in quite some time. With a boiler in the basement that was in operation around the clock, the still had a capacity of 2,800 gallons. There were seven large vats and a pair of copper columns that went up through the second floor into the attic. The device, which Edwards estimated to be worth almost $15,000, could produce 100 gallons of alcohol per day. One automobile, located near the house, contained fourteen 5-gallon cans of alcohol.[60]

The six men arrested in the raid claimed to be unemployed and all from Utica. Since none of the men was willing at that time to come forward and name the owner of the still, each of them was charged with "conspiracy in defrauding the government, manufacturing of untaxed paid distilled alcohol, setting up and distilling without bond and operation of a still without a license."[61]

NOTES

1. *Laws of the State of New York.*
2. *Chenango Weekly Advertiser*, July 26, 1811.
3. Tippetts, "Murders of Herkimer County Murders."
4. *Oyer and Terminer Minutes*, September 15, 1812.
5. *Utica (NY) Patriot*, November 10, 1812.
6. Johnson, Dictionary of America Biography, vol. 18, 472; list of prisoners pardoned and discharged from the state prison at New York, 1821.
7. *Mohawk Courier*, September 30, 1841.
8. Ibid.
9. *New York Herald*, September 29, 1841.
10. *Mohawk Courier*, September 29, 1841.
11. *New York American*, October 12, 1841.
12. Preceding quotes and this quote from coroner's inquest published by the *Utica Morning Herald*, March 28, 1883.
13. Ibid.
14. *Utica Saturday Globe*, August 22, 1903.
15. *Syracuse Journal*, August 20, 1903.
16. *Syracuse Journal*, December 24, 1903.
17. Ibid.
18. Ibid.
19. *Utica Saturday Globe*, August 22, 1903, 4.
20. *Utica Saturday Globe*, September 17, 1914.
21. Ibid., 8.
22. *Ilion News*, September 24, 1914.

23. *Rome Daily Sentinel*, October 3, 1914.
24. *Utica Herald Dispatch*, September 21, 1914.
25. *Utica Daily Press*, April 14, 1919.
26. *Utica Daily Press*, September 11, 1920.
27. *Utica Observer Dispatch*, March 31, 1920.
28. *Rome Daily Sentinel*, October 10, 1930.
29. Ibid.
30. *Rome Daily Sentinel*, September 26, 1930.
31. *Albany Times Union*, October 11, 1930.
32. *Syracuse Journal*, September 27, 1930.
33. *Utica Daily Press*, January 1, 1931.
34. *Utica Herald Dispatch*, November 27, 1911.
35. *Utica Herald Dispatch*, June 23, 1915.
36. *Utica Daily Press*, January 1, 1931.
37. *Rome Daily Sentinel*, January 8, 1931.
38. Ibid.
39. *Utica Daily Press*, January 2, 1931.
40. *Rome Daily Sentinel*, January 3, 1931.
41. *Rome Daily Sentinel*, January 5, 1931.
42. *Rome Daily Sentinel*, January 8, 1931.
43. *Utica Daily Press*, January 5, 1931.
44. *Utica Observer Dispatch*, January 5, 1931; *Rome Daily Sentinel*, January 3, 1931.
45. *Syracuse Journal*, April 15, 1931.
46. *Rome Daily Sentinel*, September 27, 1930.
47. *Utica Daily Press*, April 15, 1931.
48. Ibid.
49. *Utica Observer Dispatch*, April 15, 1931.
50. *Rome Daily Sentinel*, December 3, 1930.
51. *Utica Observer Dispatch*, April 15, 1931.
52. Ibid.
53. Ibid.
54. *Syracuse Post Standard*, April 14, 1931.
55. *Utica Daily Press*, May 31, 1933.
56. *Syracuse Journal*, April 24, 1935.
57. *Schenectady Gazette*, May 19, 1939.
58. *Rome Daily Sentinel*, August 25, 1937.
59. *Rome Daily Sentinel*, September 18, 1937.
60. *Rome Daily Sentinel*, August 25, 1937; *Utica Observer Dispatch*, August 25, 27, 1937.
61. *Utica Observer Dispatch*, August 25, 1937.

BIBLIOGRAPHY

John Adam Hartmann, the Leatherstocking Man

Herkimer County Historical Crier 31, no. 9 and 10. "Legacy" (September–October 2005).

Simms, Jeptha R. *Frontiersmen of New York.* Albany, New York: G.C. Riggs, 1882–83.

The People Versus Eleven-Year-Old John Bowman

Johnson, Allen. *Dictionary of America Biography*. Vol. 18. New York: Charles Scribner's Sons, 1929.

Laws of the State of New York. N.p.: November 10, 1812.

List of prisoners pardoned and discharged from the state prison at New York, 1821. Delaware County Clerk's Office Archival Collection.

Oyer and Terminer Circuit Minutes, 1804–1895. Herkimer County Clerk's Office, Herkimer, New York.

Murder Most Diabolical and Atrocious

Benton, Nathaniel S. *A History of Herkimer County*. Albany, NY: J. Munsell, 1856.

Herkimer Democrat. March 8, 1850.

Mohawk Courier. March 2, 14, 1850; April 11, 1850; September 17, 1850.

Tippetts, W.H. *Murders of Herkimer County*. N.p.: H.P. Wetherstone, 1885.

Utica Daily Gazette. March 8, 14, 15, 18, 19, 21, 1850; April 11, 1850.

Utica Daily Observer. March 2, 3, 4, 5, 11, 13, 1850; September 5, 6, 1850.

A Drink to Make Up

Brown, Charles P. "Descendants of Nathan Young." N.p., 1978.
Chautauqua County, New York. *Forrestville Free Press* extractions. http://chautauqua.ny.us.
Conkling, Alfred R. *Life and Letters of Roscoe Conkling*. New York: Charles L. Webster & Company, 1889.
Documents of the Senate of the State of New York, Eighty-Eighth Session, 1865. Vol. 1, nos. 1–37. Albany, NY: C. Wendell, Legislative Printer, 1865.
Executive Orders for Commutations, Pardons, Restorations and Respites, New York, 1845–1931. Ancestry.com.
Find A Grave. "Caroline Platts." www.findagrave.com.
———. "George Platts." www.findagrave.com.
———. "Mercy Wilcox." www.findagrave.com.
———. "Miles Wilcox." www.findagrave.com.
Governor's Register of Commitments to Prison, New York, 1842–1908. Ancestry.com.
Herkimer County Democrat. August 29, 1860.
———. November 13, 1861.
———. September 26, 1860.
New York State Census, 1855, 1865.
New York State Military Museum. "Civil War Units 152nd Infantry." https://dmna.ny.gov.
Roback, Henry. *New York Infantry, 152nd Regiment, 1865–1865*. Utica, NY: L.C. Childs & Sons, 1888.
Tippetts, W.H. *Murders of Herkimer County*. N.p.: H.P. Wetherstone, 1885.
U.S. Federal Census, 1850, 1860, 1870.
Utica Daily Observer. August 2, 1860.
———. September 4, 1860.
Utica Weekly Herald. September 4, 1860.

The Murder of Anson Casler

Herkimer County Journal. September 21, 28, 1865; October 5, 1865; July 12, 1871.

The Black Widow of Warren

Albany Morning Express. May 15, 1869.
Broome Republican. May 1899.
Herkimer County Citizen. May 14, 1869.

New York State Census and Death Index. Ancestry.com.
Tippetts, W.H. *Murders of Herkimer County*. N.p.: H.P. Wetherstone, 1885.

Mashed to Death

Herkimer County Democrat. August 23, 1871.
Map of the Town of Frankfort. In *Herkimer County Atlas.* New York: J. Jay Stranahan & Beach Nichols, 1868.
New York Daily Tribune. August 17, 1871.
New York Governor's Registers of Commitments to Prisons, 1842–1908.
New York State Census, 1865.
Rome Daily Sentinel. August 22, 1871.
Tippetts, W.H. *Murders of Herkimer County*. N.p.: H.P. Wetherstone, 1885.
Utica Daily Observer. August 15, 1871.
Utica Observer. August 25, 1871.
Will of Nancy Pangburn. Herkimer County Surrogates, vol. P, April 11, 1871.

Murder by the Mansion

Auburn Daily Bulletin. 1886.
Buffalo Daily Courier. 1874.
Canajoharie Radii. 1873–1918.
Davidson, Angus. *Miss Douglas of New York*. New York: Viking Press, 1953.
Executive Orders for Commutations, Pardons, Restorations and Respites, New York, 1845–1931. Ancestry.com.
Journal & Courier. 1873.
Newburg Weekly Telegram. 1874.
New York Sun. 1873.
Utica Daily Observer. 1874.

The Murders of Bellinger and Hayes

Daily Saratogian. September 27, 1889.
Little Falls Journal and Courier. "Fatal Assault in Little Falls." August 11, 1874.
———. "Law Versus 'Justice.'" December 1, 1874.
Mexico Independent. "Trial of Captain Boyd." February 8, 1890.
New York Herald. "Mysterious Murder Near Utica." August 8, 1874.
New York Times. September 27, 1889.
Oswego Daily Times. "The Boyd Case." January 25, 1890.

———. "Trial of Capt. Boyd." February 3, 1890.
Sandy Creek News. "The Mexico Murder." October 3, 1889.
———. October 17, 1889.
Syracuse Weekly Express. "Being Tried for Murder." February 6, 1890.
———. "Captain Boyd Acquitted." February 6, 1890.
Utica Daily Observer. "Two Sentences!" November 20, 1874.
Utica Morning Herald. August 8, 1874.
Waterloo Observer. "Mysterious Murder Near Utica." August 12, 1874.

The Murder of Orlo Davis

Executive Orders for Commutations, Pardons, Restorations and Respites, New York, 1884–1929. Ancestry.com.
Find A Grave. "Albert Frettenburgh (1837–13 Oct 1903). www.findagrave.com.
———. "Lodicia Underwood Fredenburg (1807–18 Jul 1884)." www.findagrave.com.
Ilion Citizen. "After 27 Years in Prison." September 4, 1903.
———. "The Fredenburg-Davis Affair." December 31, 1875.
———. May 1876.
Journal & Courier. "Body Snatching in Norway." March 28, 1876.
———. "The Fredenburgs." December 28, 1875.
———. "The Gray Murder." November 23, 1875.
———. "Horrible Murder at Gray. Orlo Davis Almost Decapitated." June 29, 1875.
———. January 4, 1876.
———. January 25, 1876.
———. July 6, 1875.
———. June 13, 1876.
———. March 23, 1876.
———. November 20, 1877.
Utica Morning Herald. "The Davis Tragedy." Tuesday, June 29, 1875.
———. "Herkimer County." Thursday, May 25, 1876.
———. "Orlo Davis Almost Decapitated." Saturday, June 26, 1875.
———. Thursday, June 8, 1876.

The Murder of Moses Craig Holden Sr.

Herkimer Democrat. August 11, 1880.
———. February 18, 1881.

The John Wishart Murder

Auburn Prison Records for Prisoners Released. Vol. 3. Series B 0068-77. Albany: New York State Archives.
Herkimer Citizen. "Murder Trial." November 21, 1884.
Little Falls Journal and Courier. "Murder in the First Degree." May 26, 1885.
New York Death Index, 1852–1956. Ancestry.com.
New York State Census, 1855, 1875, 1905.
New York Wills and Probate Records, 1659–1999. Ancestry.com.
New York, Governor's Registers of Commitments to Prisons, 1842–1908. Vol. 2. Albany: New York State Archives.
Rome Daily Sentinel. "The Mondon Trial." May 25, 1885.
Schuyler Cemetery Records. Herkimer County Historical Society.
Tippetts, W.H. *Murders of Herkimer County.* N.p.: H.P. Wetherstone, 1885.
Utica Weekly Herald. "Imprisoned for Life." December 7, 1886.

A Timeless Tragedy

Ancestry.com.
Batavia Daily News. March, 1883.
Find A Grave. www.findagrave.com.
Herkimer County Historical Society, Resources and Records. Herkimer, New York.
Herkimer Democrat. March 28, 1883, 2.
Herkimer Evening Telegram. March 31, 1883.
Oswego Palladium. 1883.
Roman Citizen. March 28, 1883.
Rome Daily Sentinel. March 30, 1883.
Utica Morning Herald. March 28, 1883.
Utica Weekly Herald. March–April, 1883.

The Hanging of a Murderess

Legacy, Annals of Herkimer County, issue no. 1 (1987). Herkimer County Historical Society.

Murder in Middleville

Herkimer Citizen. March 3, 1885; October 18, 20, 1885.

Herkimer County Clerk Records. Herkimer County Office Building, 109 Mary Street, Herkimer, New York.
Tippetts, W.H. *Murders of Herkimer County*. N.p.: H.P. Wetherstone, 1885.

Quarrel Over a Button

Amsterdam Daily Democrat. June 19, 1893.
Discharges of Convicts, 1882–1915. Ancestry.com.
Governor's Registers of Commitments to Prisons, 1842–1908. Ancestry.com.
Ilion Citizen. December 1, 1893.
———. "Platts Free Once More." September 2, 1904.
———. "Platts Murder Trial." December 15, 1893.
Johnstown (NY) Daily Republican. "Herkimer Tragedy." 1893.
New York State Census, 1865, 1892. Ancestry.com.
Rome Semi-Weekly Citizen. "The Quarrel Over a Button." June 11, 1893.
Utica Daily Observer. June 12, 17, 1893.
Utica Herald Dispatch. "James Platt Returns." August 23, 1904.

Vale of Tears

Boonville Herald. April 3, 1894.
Brooklyn Daily Eagle. May 20, 1894.
Little Falls Evening Times. April 2, 1893.
Little Falls Journal and Courier. April 3, 1894.
Utica Weekly Herald. April 3, 1894.

Jealous Lover: The Ella Ausman Murder

Canajoharie Wide-Awake Courier. April 13, 1897.
Ilion Citizen. February 5, 1897; December 23, 1898; March 4, 1898.
Journal and Courier. February 7, 1897; April 9, 1897; March 15, 1898; March 22, 1998.
Little Falls Evening Times. January 29, 30, 1897; February 1, 2, 1897.
New York Times. January 28, 1897.
Richfield Springs Mercury. March 10, 1898.
Utica Daily Union. January 29, 1897.
Utica Morning Herald. February 2, 3, 1897.
Utica Observer. February 28, 1898; March 15, 1898.
Utica Semi-Weekly Herald. January 29, 1897; February 9, 1897; April 9, 1897; September 24, 1897.

Utica Sunday Journal. January 31, 1897.
Utica Sunday Tribune. January 31, 1897; February 18, 1900.
Utica Weekly Herald. February 2, 1897.

Nellie Had a Date with Death

Ancestry.com.
Camden Advance. "Murdered at Old Forge—Nell Widrick the Victim." September 28, 1899.
Civil War Record for Solomon C. Widrig (Widrick), 32nd New York Infantry, Company E. Ancestry.com.
Federal Census, 1850, 1860, 1870, 1880, 1900, 1910 and 1920. Records for the Widrick/Widrig and Norton families.
Find A Grave. www.findagrave.com.
Governor's List of Confinements to Auburn Prison, March 1900. Ancestry.com.
Gravestones of Solomon C. Widrick and Hattie Widrick. Pineville Cemetery, Oswego County, New York.
Hough, Franklin Benjamin. *History of Lewis County, New York, with Illustrations and Biographical Sketches of Some of Its Prominent Men and Pioneers.* Syracuse, NY: D. Mason & Company, 1883. Brief biography of John Norton, father of Horace P. Norton. Also available online at Ancestry.com and https://archive.org.
Ilion Citizen. "Murder at Fulton Chain." September 28, 1899.
———. "Norton Case with the Jury." March 16, 1900.
———. "The Norton Murder Trial." March 16, 1900.
———. "The Norton Murder Trial." March 23, 1900.
Lowville Democrat. "Norton Found Guilty." March 21, 1900.
Lowville Journal and Republic. "Murdered His Paramour—Horace Norton of Glenfield Kills Miss Widrick."
New York State Archives Index of Auburn Prison Records. Reg. no. 26039, Horace P. Norton, admitted to Auburn Prison on March 19, 1900, transferred to Comstock Prison on May 16, 1916. www.archives.nysed.gov.
New York State Army Register of Enlistments for 1903. Record of Henry H. Norton's military service. Ancestry.com.
New York State Census, 1855, 1875, 1892 and 1905. Records for the Widrick/Widrig and Norton families.
New York State Deaths Register for 1925. Record for Horace P. Norton. Ancestry.com.
New York State Marriage Index, 1881–1967. Ancestry.com.

Rome Citizen. "The Norton Case." March 9, 1900.
———. Obituary notice for Solomon C. Widrick of Camden, New York. September 29, 1882.
Rome Daily Sentinel. "Horace Norton Arraigned." December 29, 1899.
Utica Herald-Dispatch. "Henry H. Norton of Port Leyden Was Mustered in Military Service." March 24, 1900.
Utica Observer. "In Terror of Norton." September 25, 1899.
———. "The Norton Case Goes to the Jury." March 15, 1900.
———. "Says Norton Made Threats." March 8, 1900.

The Case of Infanticide

Auburn Prison Statement of Commitment and Release Records, census. Ancestry.com.
Evening Times. "Hideous Depravity Case." August 11, 1902.
Find A Grave. Cemetery records. www.findagrave.com.
Ilion Citizen. "A Revolting Crime." August 15, 1902.
Utica Herald Dispatch. "Woman Was Fatally Stricken on Train." May 6, 1919.

A Rocky Marriage Ends in an Axe Blow

Census, 1880, 1892. Ancestry.com.
Evening Times. November 11, 1904.
Herkimer County Divorce Records. Herkimer County Records Room, 109 Mary Street, Herkimer, New York.
Ilion Citizen. June 25, 1908.
Rome Daily Sentinel. June 19, 1908.
Utica Herald Dispatch. June 18, 1908.

Murder on Garden Street

Amsterdam Evening Recorder. March 6, 1915.
Fort Plain Standard. April 1, 1915.
Herkimer Citizen. March 9, 30, 1915.
Little Falls Journal and Courier. March 9, 1915.
Richfield Spring (NY) Mercury. March 6, 1915.
Rome Daily Sentinel. March 6, 1915.
St. Johnsville (NY) News. March 6, 1915.
Utica Daily Press. June 4, 1915.
Utica Herald-Dispatch. March 5, 6, 9, 13, 19, 24, 1915.

Utica New York Sunday Tribune. June 27, 1915.
Utica Observer. March 6, 1915.

Caught on Film

Beacon Daily Herald. January 14, 1924.
California Death Index. Ancestry.com.
Herkimer Citizen. March 27, 1917.
Herkimer County Historical Society. "Whitehead" family file folder.
Herkimer Evening Telegram. April 9, 1917.
New York (NY) Variety. January 31, 1924.
The People of the State of New York v. Oscar Whitehead in the Matter of the Investigation as to the Insanity of Said Oscar Whitehead. May 19, 1917. Herkimer County Records Room.

A Murder of Forgiveness

Auburn (NY) Citizen. "Boy Is Indicted for Murder in First Degree in Killing Miss Beecher." April 3, 1914.
———. "Gianini Boy Confesses He Killed Miss Beecher." March 30, 1914.
———. "Motive for Crime." May 14, 1914.
———. "Now the Rebuttal." May 23, 1914.
———. "Pretty Slow Work in Jury Getting Today in Gianini Trial." May 8, 1914.
———. "School Marks Good." May 21, 1914.
———. "To Save Son's Life." May 16, 1914.
Buffalo (NY) Evening News. "Boy Murderer of Teacher Will Plead Insanity." March 31, 1914.
———. "The Sworn Confession of Jean Gianini Is Admitted in Evidence." May 14, 1914.
Goddard, Henry Herbert. *The Criminal Imbecile: An Analysis of Three Remarkable Murder Cases.* New York: MacMillan Company, 1922.
Herkimer (NY) Evening Telegram. "Again the Gianini Case." April 21, 1914.
———. "Girl Teacher Slain by Youth." April 5, 1914.
———. "Jean Gianini Is Morose at Matteawan." January 17, 1928.
———. "Jurors' Faces Are Hardened at Gianini's Confession." May 14, 1914.
Lowville (NY) Journal and Republican. "Jurymen Failed to Do Duty." June 11, 1914.
New York Sunday Tribune. "Reverend W.A. Beecher Talks of Gianini." March 31, 1914.

New York Times. "Teacher Killed Had Befriended Him." April 1, 1914.
Rome (NY) Sentinel. "Gianini Testimony All in This Week." May 22, 1914.
Schenectady (NY) Gazette. "Jean Gianini Sentenced to Matteawan." May 29, 1914.
Steuben (NY) Farmer's Advocate. "Insanity to Be Plea." April 8, 1914.
Supreme Court of Herkimer County. *The People of the State of New York v. Jean Gianini*. Transcript from stenographer's notes, vols. 1–12. Herkimer, NY, 1914.
Syracuse (NY) Journal. "Boy Slayer Makes Clean Breast of Crime to Coroner." March 30, 1914.
———. "Jean Gianini Knew What He Was Doing." May 22, 1914.
———. "Jurors Disregard County's Protest." June 26, 1914.
———. "She 'Snitched' So I Killed Her, Says Boy Slayer." May 19, 1914.
———. "Slain Girl's Bloody Garments in Court." May 12, 1914.
———. "State to Open Guns Upon Young Slayer." May 23, 1914.
Utica (NY) Daily Press. "Boy Is Held for Murder." March 30, 1914.
———. "Defense Closed Its Case Today." May 23, 1914.
———. "Did Not Know Exact Nature of Crime." May 22, 1914.
———. "Gianini Heard Murder Described." May 12, 1914.
———. "Selecting the Jury in the Gianini Case." May 5, 1914.
———. "Waiting for the Verdict in Murder Case." May 28, 1914.
Utica (NY) Saturday Globe. "Queries Hypothetic." May 23, 1914.

The Notorious 1916 Little Falls Trunk Murder

Buckley, Richard. *Unique Place, Diverse People: The Social and Political History of Little Falls*. N.p., 2008.
Little Falls Evening Times. July 26, 2000.
Little Falls Journal and Courier. January 2, 1917.
———. November 7, 1916.

The Killing of Henry Werner

Albany Times Union. "Rutger Warder Funeral Today." October 29, 1963.
Federal Census, 1930. Ancestry.com.
Find A Grave. "Jennie C Hills (1889–1981)." www.findagrave.com.
Knickerbocker News. "Rutger B. Warder." October 29, 1963.
New York Evening World. "Werner Slaying Opens New Clues." February 25, 1921.
New York State Death Index, 1957–1968. Ancestry.com.

Rome Daily Sentinel. "Governor Commutes Warder Sentence to Life Imprisonment." January 25, 1923.
———. "State Closes Werner Case, Defense Opens." May 5, 1927.
Thomas E. Dewey Papers. University of Rochester, River Campus Libraries, Special Collections. Series 7, Box 119, Folder 2, Clemency, 1947–49.
Utica Daily Press. "Frankfort Notes." Thursday, June 7, 1923.
———. "Ilion Murder Case May Solve the Kelley and Dade Crimes." February 24, 1921.
Utica Herald-Dispatch. "Jennie Werner's Fate Is Now in Hands of Jurors." May 11, 1921.
Utica Morning Telegram. "Mrs. Werner's Mother Knows Who Killed Albert Dade." May 5, 1921.
———. "Warder Asked About Kelley Death Mystery." February 25, 1921.
———. "Warder Cries Out Warning to Mrs. Werner." February 26, 1921.
———. "Warder Tells Court Why He Turned Against Widow of Murdered Man." May 5, 1921.
Utica Observer Dispatch. September 27, 1933.

A Wolf in Sheep's Clothing

Albany Evening Journal. 1924.
Amsterdam Evening Recorder. 1924.
Brookfield Courier. 1900.
Brown, Charles P. "Descendants of Cora Firman & John House." In *The Descendants of Nathan Young.* N.p.: privately printed, 1978.
Cooperstown Freeman's Journal. 1900, 1920, 1924.
Evening Times. 1924.
Fulton Patriot. 1921.
Herkimer Evening Telegram. 1924.
Lowville Journal. 1924.
Richfield Springs Mercury. 1883–1924.
Shults, L.H. *The Haus (House) Family of the Mohawk.* N.p.: privately printed, 1968.
Syracuse Evening Herald. 1900.
Syracuse Evening Telegram. 1900.
Syracuse Journal. 1924.
Syracuse Post Standard. 1901.
Utica Daily Press. 1902, 1905–1907, 1909–1910, 1913, 1918–1919, 1922, 1924.
Utica Daily Union. 1896.
Utica Herald-Dispatch. 1900, 1906–1907, 1912–1916.

Utica Observer. 1900.
Utica Observer-Dispatch. 1924.
Utica Sunday Journal. 1896, 1905.
Utica Sunday Tribune. 1902, 1907.
Utica Weekly Herald. 1895
Watertown Daily Times. 1924.
Will of J.H. House, 1924. Book 48, p. 307. Surrogate's Office, Herkimer County, New York.

Wagner-Hotaling Murder of Little Falls

Ancestry.com.
Auburn Citizen. September 1, 1926.
Evening Times. September 1, 1926; December 28, 29, 30, 31, 1926.
Find A Grave. www.findagrave.com.
Schenectady Gazetteer. December 29, 1926.
Utica Daily Press. December 29, 1926.
———. September 4, 1926.
Utica Observer Dispatch. December 31, 1927.
———. January 12, 1927.

The Final Argument

Herkimer Telegram-Record. May 3, 1927.

The Trespassing Cows

Albany (NY) Evening Journal. March 21, 1931.
Buffalo Courier Express. March 22, 1931.
Jamestown Evening Journal. November 11, 1930.
Kinderhook (NY) Advertiser. March 27, 1931.
New Berlin (NY) Gazette. December 4, 1930.
Otsego Farmer. January 17, 1930.
Syracuse American. March 22, 1931.
U.S. Census, 1910, 1940. Ancestry.com.
Utica Daily Press. January 31, 1928.

ABOUT THE EDITORS

Caryl Hopson has been with the Herkimer County Historical Society for twenty-seven years in an administrative capacity, overseeing programs, projects, exhibits and fundraising activities for the organization, including a recent collaboration with the local theater company Ilion Little Theatre in the production of a new play, *Shattered Angel*, written by Stephen Wagner, about the famous 1914 Jean Gianini murder, as well as a previous play, *Roxy*, written by Jack Sherman and based on the 1884 Roxalana Druse murder.

Susan Perkins has been with the Herkimer County Historical Society for thirty-six years as an archivist, administrative assistant and, for the past twenty-two years, the executive director. She writes monthly articles for the *Mohawk Valley Living* magazine on the area's history and serves as the town of Manheim historian.

Together they have worked with Arcadia Publishing on four publications for the "Images of America" series: *Herkimer Village*, *German Flatts*, *Frankfort* and *Little Falls*.

www.ingramcontent.com/pod-product-compliance
Lightning Source LLC
Chambersburg PA
CBHW060343100426
42812CB00003B/1109